Facing the Flames

All the best
Connie Brown

Also by Connie O'Brien

Where It Was Hot

Facing the Flames

by

Connie O'Brien

dmc books
Dover, NH

Copyright © 2001 by Connie O'Brien

published by
dmc associates, inc.
PO Box 1095
Dover, NH 03821-1095

All rights reserved. No part of this work may be reproduced or transmitted in any form whatsoever exept for brief passages that may be used by a reviewer. Requests for permissions should be addressed to the publisher.

ISBN: 1-8798-22-8

Printed in the United States of America

First Printing

Contents

Smokey Joe—11
Part of the Job—16
Plenty of Sauce—19
A Screaming Lady—23
The Roundhouse Fire—26
Apple Pie with the Chief—30
The Major—34
Barrel Factory Fire—36
A Firefighter's Dilemma—40
Have a Cigar—42
A Christmas Fire—44
Voting—47
Sunday Mass—49
Golden Memories—51
A Toy Factory—57
Duff Springs—60
Cott Bottling Plant—62
Dimmick Street—67
Armory Fire—70
Officer Mulligan—75
Holes in My Lids—77
A Boat Ride—79
The Harvard Lampoon—83
Hot Pipes—87
Sledding, Anyone?—91
Mineral Spirtis Fire—94
Captain Foley's New Toy—99
Jordan Marsh Warehouse—102
The Last Day of Study—106
A Visist—110
Bones—112
Fire Down Under—114

Wine & Cheese—119
A Funeral Fire—121
Our Neighbor—124
An Unfunny Valentine—127
The Prison Point Bridge Fire—131
The Aku Aku—138
A View from the Window—143
Green Street—145
An International Incident—150
Sizzle in the Snow—152
The East Boston Fires—155
Baby Doll—159
The Vendome—161
Benny—165
Ice Cream—167
Leroy—170
Caught in a Storm—175
Can You Play the Spoons?—178
A Dash of Radiation—181
A Twinkle in his Eye—184
A Room Full of Candles—186
Jesse—189
A Fish Story—193
A Request—198
A Noise—203
A Love Story—206
A Tug of War—209
The Worcester Fire—212

Dedication

I would like to dedicate this book to all the faces that are with me now only in memory. Some were family, some were firefighters, others were dear friends. All played an important part in my life.

I like to believe that we all will meet again in a place where tragedy and pain are unknown and happiness and health prevail.

All these faces have names and a fading power of memory has stored them in a special place. There they will stay until we all meet one day at the big one in the sky.

Connie O'Brien
May 1, 2001

Facing the Flames

Smokey Joe

I suspect that when we are young most of us tend to attach ourselves to someone who seems to know the ropes. From the very first minute that I met Smokey Joe I knew that he was an expert in the business of firefighting. Physically he was not a big man. His face resembled a punched out boxer, and this may have made him appear larger than he actually was.

The first night on the job I was a bundle of nerves. Smokey knew what I was going through. We watched the eleven o'clock news and then it was time to hit the bunk room. The lieutenant had shown me my bed earlier in the tour. In those days we used rubber coated pants that folded over our short boots. Suspenders were attached to the pants. The boots had an attached ring, a boot hitch, that enabled you to pull the boots on more easily. This entire rig was called a *night hitch*. When an alarm came in during the night you would swing your legs into the boots, use the hitch's ring to pull them up and put the suspenders on and then you were ready to run down the hall to the sliding pole.

After placing the hitch next to my bunk, I sat there wondering if I would cut the mustard. Joe knew how I felt. He checked my hitch and said, "All you have to do, kid, is follow the leader." In those days masks were a specialty item worn only by the Rescue Company. There was a dim light in the hall and I could hear the man on floor patrol talking to someone. My eyes were wide open and I heard every creak in that old building. My senses were sharp and straining to hear the striker hitting the gong. Finally, I dozed off. The gong was sounding; the house lights were on. My eyes snapped open and into my night hitch, I jumped. Now I was running down the hall toward the pole. Joe was running after me to inform me that it was an uptown box and we did not have to go. The house lights went out and as I walked back to my bunk I could hear the unmistakable sound of snickering. After about five minutes the lights came on again and this time the bells were sounding the all out signal. It had been a false alarm. Sleep was impossible for the remainder the night. The next morning around the coffee table I took some kidding: "How'd ya sleep, Obie?" and "Did you guys hear any one running down the hall?"

I swear that Joe could breathe smoke. About six weeks after I was appointed we had an attic fire. We were second company and the chief ordered us to make the attic and back up a company that was in front of us. They were huddled at a turn of the stairs leading to the attic. Joe told them to advance the line but they were not moving. He now actually started to crawl over them and up the stairs. Well, if he could do it so can I, I thought, and so over the boys I advanced. Joe was now at the top landing yelling, "Light up on the line, Obie!" which meant give him more hose. Unfortunately, I couldn't breathe at this point. The smoke was choking me to death as if someone had a hand on my windpipe and was squeezing tighter and tighter. Joe was now yelling for me to take out a window. I looked ahead and saw something that looked like a window. With my helmet, I tried to break out the glass. Repeatedly I smashed the helmet against it. Why won't it break? I kept asking myself. Later I learned that it was a mirror. If the smoke hadn't been so thick I would have had a good look at myself.

Meanwhile, Joe had moved further down the hall. Hot water

was cascading down on me, running down my neck and burning the hell out of me. The fire involved one room at the end of the hall. Joe held the line against the ceiling. Soon the fire was knocked down and we started to overhaul. Joe said that we should go out and "take a blow", which I somehow translated to mean "get some air". Other guys were now in the room where Joe and I had been working, and I saw him glance at the mirror as we passed. I did not say a word and Smokey Joe never mentioned it.

I suppose the guys we crawled over were a little put out but Joe was determined to get at that fire. That man could take a fantastic amount of smoke. I suppose every fire department had a Smokey Joe or two, but his type is long gone. Today's firefighters are much more knowledgeable about the insidious components of smoke. In the leather lung days we dealt mainly with wood smoke. There were chemical fires but not like the products of combustion today.

Five years and many fires later I decided to give the lieutenant's test a try. Smokey had taken at least four tests previously but failed to pass. His problem was the mathematics required in the hydraulic questions. One night I was studying in the kitchen when he sat down beside me and asked how it was going. I asked him if he was interested in the test. With a wave of his hand, he replied, "I got no luck with exams, Connie." It took some convincing but finally I was able to get him up to my house for some study sessions. A whiz at hydraulics I was not, but I did have a basic understanding of how to apply the formulas. We sat at my dining room table and went over and over the work. Joe was having a hard time remembering the correct formulas and how to apply them.

There were other things to remember, like the twenty-two reasons that cellar fires were hard to fight. We developed a code, which was a method to remember by association. For example, the code for "difficult to ventilate" was "When your father came home from work and took his socks off, every one got sick." The memory click here was the idea that you had to get the odor out of the house, you had to *ventilate*. The more ridiculous they were the better. We would sit there and laugh. The funnier they were the better chance of remembering them.

The morning of the exam Joe sat three seats away from me. Before we went in I told him to stay cool and it would be fine. All he needed was a decent passing grade and due to his experience mark, he should get promoted. About an hour into the test I glanced his way and noted that he was in trouble. Suddenly he stood up and tore the papers. There was nothing that I could do. Joe never took another test. After I was promoted I moved on to other assignments and, being assigned to other groups, we never worked together again. He had taught me much about the profession of firefighting.

I was a lieutenant assigned to Engine 6 in the south side of Cambridge. One morning I reported to duty and was informed that there had been a terrible fire on Cambridge Street near Engine 5. Smokey Joe had been acting lieutenant. In those days, when an officer was absent, the senior man working would take charge of the company. It was also Joe's last tour of duty before his retirement. At about three o'clock in the morning a trailer truck was headed up Cambridge Street and the driver saw flames blowing out a second floor window of a four story taxpayer—a structure with commercial space on the ground floor and residences above—on the Cambridge Street side. No one was around that hour of the morning so the driver drove the half a block to the station and sounded his air horn. Smokey Joe struck a second alarm on arrival, ordered a line to cover the front exit stairs, and was responsible for the rescue of five people over ladders. It was a freezing cold morning in early March. We relieved the Engine 6 crew at the fire. Unfortunately, three little children had lost their lives. They were gone before Engine 5 arrived at the scene. When I found Joe, he was sitting on the rear step of a hose wagon. His bloodshot eyes and running nose told it all. He looked at me and said, "Connie, I tried my best to get them all out...." There was nothing for me to say. The proper words failed to come. All that I could do was give him a hug and whisper, "It's OK, Joe. It's OK." We sat there as they removed the children in body bags. It was a moment I will always remember. My company was dismissed from the fire and we put the frozen hose on top of the hose wagon. Back at the station a cup of hot coffee tasted very good. The hose wagon was repacked and the frozen hose was left in a pile in the rear of the pump.

Smokey Joe's retirement party was held in a hall in East Cambridge with jakes from Cambridge, Somerville, Boston and points beyond attending. We roasted and toasted Joe until three in the morning. I heard some years later that Smokey had passed away up in Portland, Maine. I am sure that when Joe finally met his God, he was greeted with the words, "Come to me, my good and faithful servant! You were a firefighter."

Part of the Job

On hot summer nights the firehouse was definitely not the most comfortable place to be. This tour had been normal for a Saturday night. We had our regular run of false alarms early in the night, the same boxes that were pulled with regularity—Kelly School, Washington Street between the housing projects, Windsor and School, Houghton and Oak. Often we'd go from one false alarm to another. Obviously the culprits never considered the dangers they created for firefighters or the fact that if a legitimate fire broke out at any time, there could be a delay in response.

I had the ten to midnight watch and hit the sack about one. It's funny how sound carries on a hot sultry night. The people next door were having an argument about who would be invited to a wedding. Outside my window was a flat roof where we stretched out hose to dry. This roof connected to just under the second story window sill of the adjoining three story tenement on Inman Street, so as I sat on my bed looking left, my line of vision was into their kitchen.

The argument was heating up and the language was getting foul. Finally someone yelled, "Cut the shit and invite the sonuvabitch to the fucken wedding so we can get some sleep." Now there was mumbling, followed by silence, then their kitchen light went out so I guess they ran out of steam.

At 3:00 a.m. the house lights came on and the bells jumped

to life. A box for Cambridge and Tremont Streets was coming in. It was only three blocks from the station. Riding the rear step of the wagon, I could see the haze of smoke up the street. We had a fire! The pumper took a hydrant and Lieutenant Magee was giving me the hand signal to drop a big line. Now I could both hear and see the fire. The flames were reflecting against the house next door. Overlapping fire was igniting the frame dwelling less than eight feet away.

Lieutenant Magee had already notified Fire Alarm that we had a working fire. Billy was holding the hose while I tried to screw the playpipe on the line. The one holding the hose almost feels compelled to try to help the one attaching the pipe; of course, sometimes this only creates more problems as it makes it hard to catch the threads. We carried twelve lengths of two and a half inch hose on the left rear of the wagon and twelve on the right. The lengths were connected together, then separated as needed to reach the fire. Finally the pipe was on and I headed toward the front door. I could hear people screaming and the sound of breaking glass. There was a dull thud beside me and I looked down to see the body of a large woman. She had jumped from an upper floor. She was not moving and her head seemed to be crushed.

Other companies were now arriving and going to work. As I dragged the line toward the stairs I saw him. He was impaled on the picket fence in front of the house. The pickets had gone through him; he was still moving. The line was charged and we directed it at the ceiling of the stairs. From the landing above me people began tumbling down the stairs. The fire was not far behind them.

Chief O'Connor had ordered a second alarm. The proximity of other buildings created the real danger that the fire would spread. Soon an engine company had a line working on the exposure. It didn't take much time to knock down the overlapping fire. Two men from the Rescue Company passed us on the stairs and conducted a search of the second and third floors. We held the line against the ceiling to cool things down.

The upper floors were clear. The only people were those who had tumbled past us on the stairs. Lieutenant Magee said, "It's down boys, let's take a blow." Out front the Rescue guys were removing the body from the fence. They had cut a section of the fence to remove the victim. He had been transported to the Cambridge City Hospital with the fence still in him. Due to massive internal injuries there was little that they could do. The lady who had jumped had already been taken away. There was blood everywhere.

After a smoke, we assisted in overhauling the second and third floors. Later we learned that the sixteen year old boy had leaped from the third floor attic front window. The fire had started in the second floor apartment of the lady who jumped. The three people who were able to get to the front stairs were occupants of a rear apartment. We used an inch and a half line to wash the blood down the sewer.

The sun was rising when we backed into quarters. A light was on in the doughnut shop, and I knew Saul would be making his doughnuts. After throwing all the wet hose off the wagon step we loaded dry hose on. The calling out of the numbers stamped on the couplings had a mater-of-fact monotone and then there was silence, a silence I had heard before, a silence that was becoming familiar.

I sat on the edge of the bed in the bunk room. I knew sleep would be impossible. When I walked into the loafing room, Lennie, the cop who had the last half duty tour, sat looking out at the square. "Tough one tonight, Connie?" I answered, "Yes." The traffic was starting to build and Lennie stood up and tussled my hair saying, "It's all part of the job, kid. It's all part of the job."

Plenty of Sauce

I was sweeping the floor upstairs at Engine 5 when the lieutenant answered the house phone. He was now shaking the sliding pole and informing me that I was next on the detail list and they were looking for a man to go to the Rescue Company for the day. Great, I said to myself as I answered him in my sweetest voice, "OK, Lieutenant. I got it." This would be an exciting tour. The Rescue Company was busy and answered all alarms for a reported fire. They were also sent out of town occasionally on mutual aid assignments. I was in my fourth month on the fire department and always looking for action.

The regular Rescue officer had called in sick and Sonny Flynn was acting lieutenant. "Hey, kid, have you been detailed up here before?" I answered that this was my first time. Sonny was a well seasoned firefighter and had been attached to the Rescue for quite some time. "Just keep your nose clean, kid, and stay out of the way...OK, kid?"

The Rescue normally runs with a five man crew including the officer. At the time they were the only unit that would regularly wear masks. We had masks on the engine company, but for the most part they stayed in the box. I guess we thought it was just more manly not to wear them. Get in there and take a beating was the thing to do.

Our first run came at about 9:00 a.m. we were told to meet the police on Soden Street for a man who had not been heard from for a few days. When we arrived the police were already there and waiting for us. It was a first floor apartment and we used a Halligan bar to force the window open. The instant the window went up the smell almost knocked Sonny over. He said, "Oh boy, we have a ripe one in here." He was right. The man had died in bed alone and unattended. I guess he had no family left and lived alone. It was late August and the temperature, even in the morning, was high. The police took charge of the incident from that point and we returned to quarters.

Bobby Conrad was driving and Sonny was next to him. He leaned back and asked, "Hey do you guys want to stop for doughnuts?" The thought of doughnuts did not appeal to me. I didn't cast my vote and we picked up two dozen for the boys at headquarters. I was helping to clean tools when the next call came in. It was about 11:00 a.m. Three of us sat in the back of the Rescue and the driver and officer were up front. As we rocked down Cambridge Street, Sonny was yelling over the roar of the Federal siren that this call was for a person hit by a train in the freight yard. In the East Cambridge section of the city there is a huge freight yard, part of which is in Somerville and separated from Boston by the Charles River lower basin. The way the tracks were laid out, it was impossible to get very close to the accident. We could see people standing off in the distance in the maze of tracks. Sunny assigned me to carry the case containing medical supplies. The other guys grabbed various pieces of equipment. As we crossed the tracks one of the guys was saying, "I suppose this is a meat job." Bobby answered, "Them fuckin' cops always want us to clean up the fuckin' mess." As we drew close to the scene I remember getting a strange feeling of apprehension. What was I about to see? I wanted to act as tough as the other guys. The victim was a man. The train had cut him completely in half. The torso was about fifteen feet away from the rest of the body. We used blankets to cover both halves. One by one the police left the scene. The railroad cops remained with us while we waited for the medical examiner to arrive. They had a lousy track record. No matter how I tried, my eyes kept returning to the body. It was like a magnet drawing me to it.

"Hey, how the hell long are we supposed to stay here?"

The cop answered Sonny, "You guys can leave any time that you want."

We left the blankets covering the remains. The hospital would provide us with others.

We were stopped at a red light on Columbia Street when Sonny poked his head into the rear cab and yelled, "Hey, should we stop at Rocco's for subs?" Everyone was enthusiastic about the suggestion—except me. My stomach was still dealing with the freight yard. Bobby stayed with the rescue to monitor any calls we might get while we went into Rocco's. I was the last one through the door. It was around noon and the place was very busy; many of the workers from the factories in the area picked up subs for their lunch. Sonny was the first to order: "Tony, my lad, give be a meatball sub, OK! And put extra sauce on it." I was still standing near the door and because it was crowded no one noticed the green tint was creeping over my face. One by one my brother firefighters ordered meatball subs.

Tony dipped the ladle deep into the sauce and heaped it on the meatballs. I was getting greener by the minute. Now it was my turn to order. I felt that every eye in the store was on me. In the strongest voice that I could muster, my large meatball sub was ordered. However, no matter how hard I tried I could not say the words "extra sauce."

The ride back to the station was uneventful. Without hesitation the good old boys made their way to the kitchen on the third floor. The news at noon was on the television. We sat there and watched the latest happenings in the world. The small talk was flowing. Sonny offered a running commentary as he devoured his meatball sandwich: "Oh boy, this is really tasty... Mmmmm...Just the way I like it...plenty of sauce. Rocco makes a great sub, huh!" The other guys were similarly enjoying their lunch. Me, I just sat there and forced myself to eat. With every bite my stomach did flip flops. "Connie, how'd ya like the sub?" I just looked at Sonny and gave him a weak smile. Trying to act as nonchalant as I possibly could, I made my way down to the boiler room. After finding the coal pile, I dug a hole with my hand and deposited my red meatball sub. As I stood there in a cold sweat I wondered if I would ever qualify as a fireman. Maybe I ought to resign and get another job.

Of course, later in my career when I looked back at this incident, it was quite clear that my big brave fellow workers were just as bothered by the tragic incident as I was. They, in their own way, were telling me something. The lesson was to try to leave the trauma where you find it. Firefighters have feelings just like everyone else. The only difference is that they do the job that they are paid to do.

A Screaming Lady

To enter a burning building alone and inexperienced is asking for trouble. When I was appointed to the Cambridge Fire Department, I was instructed to stay close to the officer. In most cases this is what I did. There is no margin for error within a smoke filled building. To get turned around is easy. It can mean disaster once you lose the direction to the outside. An experienced man will be very careful not to be confused when the visibility becomes zero. Even before the building is entered the location of doors and windows will be noted from the outside. Before a window is entered a hook or the tip of the playpipe will be used to find if there is a floor. Once in the building a slow creeping or crawling posture will be employed. There could be open elevator pits or holes cut in the floor for various reasons. The lieutenant would take off his glove and wave his bare hand in the air to test the heat build-up over our heads. Masks were few and far between back in those days. You were supposed to eat the smoke and that was that. The final word was always, as it is today, *caution*. I was extremely fortunate in that respect because I always worked with an experienced crew.

I had just finished mopping the upstairs loafing room when the alarm of fire came in. As I hung on the back of the hose wagon I could see the smoke in the distance. It looked like it was coming from the factory district down off Cambridge Street. It was jet black and pulling hard. This rapid rise means that there is plenty of heat building up. The fire was in a two story combination office and factory complex that dealt in steel drums. The lieutenant was signaling for me to drop a big line. We were first due, but help was on the way. The fire originated in the shop area on the first floor but had already extended to the second floor. As I pulled the two and a half inch line from the wagon an explosion nearly knocked me off my feet. Fifty five gallon drums were flying through the air over our heads. We advanced the line into the storage yard. I was on the pipe and Billy and the lieutenant were backing me up. The shop area was a solid sea of flame. The line was charged and we directed the stream onto the seat of the fire. To our left I could see an office area. It was during working hours and there would be a work force in the building.

Ladder companies had arrived and were going into search, venti-lation and rescue operations. Other companies were now getting into operation. The chief was at the scene and already ordered a working fire.

We were ordered to advance the big line over a thirty five foot ladder to the roof of the one story extension. We had no sooner made the roof than a peculiar noise started to come from within the factory. It was a low key wail, unlike anything that I had ever heard. We were behind a roof extension of a fire wall about four feet high. The wail was now more pronounced and piercing. Now I recognized it. Women were inside and making the mournful plea to be rescued. Yes, that's it! There were people in there who needed to be rescued. Without hesitation I started to leave the security of the wall and jump to the rescue. The firm strong hand of the lieutenant grabbed me and pulled me back. Now the crescendo of the screams was almost deafening. He yelled into my ear, "Keep your head down!" Then it happened. The explosion actually lifted us off the tarpapered roof. We now directed a fog water pattern over our heads and I pulled my helmet tighter down over my ears. A gigantic ball of fire rose into the air. Even though the fog protected us I still felt the extreme heat. Voices from down below were now yelling to us to vacate the roof. With some difficulty we were able to bull the charged line down the ladder. The fire now was a full second alarm. It now had full control of the garage and office area on the second floor. I was ordered to get a hose clamp and run our line into our wagon deck gun. There were other exposions, some of which were severe.

The fire burned for about two hours before being declared under control. The chief ordered us to make up our lines. I asked the lieutenant about the fate of the screaming people. He smiled and shook his head from side to side: "Connie, what you heard was superheated air escaping from the vent holes in the top of the drums. They probably contained alcohol or something. If you'd gone over the wall you would've gotten it right in the kisser."

That night after supper I lay on the parlor couch staring at the ceiling. I guess I wasn't acting like myself because Peggy asked me what was wrong. I replied that everything was fine, just another day at the office. Before I went to sleep that night I thanked God for the hand of experience that pulled me back and saved my life.

THE ROUNDHOUSE FIRE

Paid details were far and few between. Occasionally you would get a detail for a live production of a play or a concert at one of Harvard's or MIT's theaters or larger auditoriums, or maybe a detail at a demolition site. We were marking hose for identification purposes at large fires when the lieutenant called me to the office and said that there was a detail available down the freight yard for the following day, Thursday. I jumped at the opportunity. Detail money was excellent and in many cases you didn't have to stay at the detail for the whole day.

I called Engine 3 in the afternoon and told them that I had the detail for the next day. They told me that there were six lengths of inch and a half, a reducer connection, playpipe and hydrant wrench waiting for me. They also told me to wash the hose when I was finished. If the detail lasted more than one day it was mine as long as I was not scheduled to be on duty.

Major renovations were being undertaken in the freight yard as part of a long range plan for an extension to Boston's infamous Southeast Expressway. This would take traffic around and under the city. In the freight yard there was a massive wood and steel roundhouse where the trains were turned around. There was also a repair shop where trains had been serviced years ago. Much of the area was now abandoned. Many of the old buildings were already demolished.

The demolition company had a curious record of having

major fires at their job sites. Maybe it was just a coincidence, but it did seem that whereever they had the contract to demolish a building a major fire would occur. The day of my detail was cool, sunny, with a gentle breeze blowing from the southwest, the fair wind direction. It was an ideal day for a burn. After picking up the hose and other equipment and receiving another warning to wash the hose, I reported to the freight yard. There was the boss of the burn. He was about six feet tall with a healthy tan and a serious look on his face. As I walked toward him I got the sense that ours was to be strictly a business arrangement. The area where the burn was to take place was wide open. About one half of the roundhouse was already down. There was a good yard hydrant located nearby and pressure would be no problem. The boss of the burn had arranged three piles of timbers. These piles were each at least fifty feet high. In my best authoritative voice—which was cracking just a bit—I asked him what were his intentions. He gave me a look like I was a grammar school kid, placed his face near mine and said, "We intend to burn them."

Rising up to my full five foot six stature I replied, "No you won't, because the piles are too high and too close together."

His reply was quick: "Am I going to have trouble with you?"

My reply was just as curt: "Bet your ass you are." Then I saw him. He was a little man and was carrying the kind of oil can the old locomotive engineers used to lubricate the moving components of the train. He was lubricating the timbers with gasoline—a squirt here and a squirt there. At the top of my voice I yelled at him but he refused to hear me. He was dancing around like a banshee of old between the piles, squirting here and there. There was a sinister smile on his face as much to say, "I have the gas! Catch me if you can."

My original intention was to have two low piles and start the pile going downwind. This could be controlled with my hose line. The best of plans can go awry. Somehow the pile closest to the wind got going. It may have been the boss of the burn, or rats and matches, or it may have been my little pal with the gas can. We will never know, but now there was work afoot.

The fire was spreading rapidly. Great clouds of acrid black smoke were rising into the clear blue sky. It's been said the smoke was visible far out at sea, half way to Ireland. There was no more time to catch the gas can guy, so I started my woefully inadequate efforts to control the fire. Now all three piles were going. The great waves of heat were presenting me with the choice of abandoning my position or becoming a cinder.

Now the wind changed direction. The standing shell of the roundhouse was smoking. I yelled to the boss of the burn to pull the hook on the fire alarm box out on the street, but he either was ignoring me or could not hear me over the roar of the flames. I could see the oil can man through the heat waves dancing gleefully among the burning piles. My line was doing absolutely nothing. I could hear the sound of sirens clearly now. It would be like a firemen's convention. Boston was first to arrive. Next came Cambridge, followed closely by Somerville. Each had three engines, two trucks and a chief or two.

There, standing beside me was the Cambridge division deputy chief. To say that he didn't look happy would be putting it lightly. If looks could kill I would have been buried last week and without the melodic strains of bagpipes. He was so angry that his voice was cracking over the roaring flames: "What the good Jesus is going on here?"

My reply was kind of a stutter, whimper, and groan. "Chief, it was the little guy with the oil can, Chief." I am sure that he would have said more but it was reported to him that the fire had spread into the remaining section of the roundhouse. All the chiefs were issuing orders and I resumed my chase after the runt with the can. Somerville now was striking a second alarm. Logan Airport called Fire Alarm and wanted to know how long they would have to alter the approach to the runways. In his haste to get away from me, the can man dropped the can and was making tracks out of the area. The boss of the burn was long gone; he probably quit.

Deck guns were working, headway was being made. It took about two hours to darken the fire down. I assisted the companies in making up hose which had been laid across and under tracks. I guess someone had told the chief about the demolition company's track record because he was nowhere near as angry as before. He just pointed his finger at me and said, "I want a full written report from you."

Meanwhile, back at Engine 3, the members were waiting for me when I returned the hose. The lieutenant was standing there with his arms folded. *"Wash the damned hose!"* he yelled. My face was bright red from the heat and even with second degree burns I managed a tired smile. The hose was washed and hung to dry.

Apple Pie with the Chief

Wednesday was inspection day. This meant that the company would go out of service at about nine in the morning and conduct inspections of dwellings in our inspection district. We would stay out until about eleven thirty or so. Another company would cover any runs in our district. In the event of a working fire or multiple alarm, we would be called and would go back into service.

This Wednesday was a fine early summer day. There was no sign of rain, which would have kept us in quarters. With open cabs in both the pump and the wagon it would be difficult to keep the paperwork dry. Each street address had a separate card. When the inspection was complete, the date and the conditions would be noted. Serious infractions would demand immediate action. Back in those days many people were heating and cooking with range oil. This fuel was normally stored in fifty five gallon drums in the basement. Range oil was lugged up to the apartment in three gallon cans. Many times oil was splashed on the wooden rear stairs leading from the basement. When fire coming from the cellar hit those oil soaked stairs it was a virtual blowtorch.

We were on Maple Avenue. The lieutenant would assign each man a group of five cards with addresses. I noted a slight snicker on the lieutenant's face. As I glanced at the cards I noted that the chief of the department's house was on the list.

"Hey, that's the chief's house! Do we inspect it?" I was a real rookie and only on the job a short time, but even with my limited service, inspecting a chief's home did not sit right. More snickering—this time by Maloney and Kelly. The lieutenant assured me that the chief would be honored to have his house inspected. I argued further but to no avail.

As I rang the chief's doorbell the anticipation was building within me. What would he say? Would he yell at me? Would he order me out of his yard? A woman answered the bell and said, "Hello!" She smiled and looked over my shoulder at the apparatus, then asked, "What can I do for you?"

I sheepishly announced, "I'm here to inspect the premises, ma'am."

She replied, "Oh I see," and called over her shoulder, "Tim, there's a fireman here to inspect the house...Come in, come in and what is your name?" she asked.

"Hoseman O'Brien," I replied.

Now the chief was standing behind her. He was also looking at the apparatus out on the street. "Well, what would like to see first?" he asked, then immediately said, "Let's start in the basement." I had heard that the chief was an amateur furniture finisher. Down we went into the chief's workshop, which was virtually spotless. Each can was in order and neatly stored in metal cabinets. "You should see my permits for the storage of flammable fluids, Hoseman," he said. Everything was in perfect order. Now he insisted that I see how he stripped and refinished wood. He explained every aspect of the hobby to me in detail; however, my mind was focused on the fact that I had already been in the house for forty five minutes. When he was finished showing me all the beautifully crafted furniture he had completed, his wife was waiting for us upstairs. Now the remainder of the home was to be inspected. As we passed through the kitchen I could see my fellow firefighters sitting on the running board of the apparatus, awaiting my return. The lieutenant was looking at his watch as the noon hour was rapidly approaching.

Now I thanked the chief and his wife and was heading for the door. The chief, however, had another plan: "Ella, Hoseman O'Brien is having lunch with us," he announced.

"Oh! How nice," she replied. "I'll set the table for three."

Hoseman O'Brien, of course, did not want to stay for lunch. Hoseman O'Brien wanted to go back to the apparatus. I tried to say thanks but no thanks, but met with no success. The course was set; I would lunch with the chief and his wife. We all sat down at the kitchen table. When I glanced out the window I could see the lieutenant standing and glaring at the house.

The lunch was delicious. We had cold chicken sandwiches on dark rye and pickles. I couldn't help thinking that I was in a pickle. Now I started to get up and leave the table. The lieutenant had moved closer to the house and I could see the look on his face. The chief was also looking at him though the window; he was glaring too. Woe is I!

It was time to go now. I thanked them for the lunch and tour of their home, but the boys were waiting for me. Then I saw it—a homemade apple pie was cooling on top of the stove. "Hoseman O'Brien," said the chief, "you must stay and have a piece of my wife's pie." The lieutenant was now having a fit and in heated conference with the boys outside. I stated in my finest apologetic voice that I should rejoin the troops, but the chief had other plans. Looking directly at me, so that there would be no mistake in my understanding, he said in no uncertain terms, **"You will have some of Ella's apple pie!"**

Down I sat as the kitchen window was opened and the sweet fragrance of freshly baked apple pie gently drifted through the window to find and caress the nostrils of my hungry and anxious fellow firemen.

Finally we were finished. I thanked the chief and his most gracious wife for the lovely lunch. Now it was time to face the lieutenant. I had been gone for one hour and ten minutes. As I approached the apparatus it was obvious that the lieutenant was talking to himself. He continued to mumble and shrug his shoulders for the remainder of the tour. No further mention was ever made to me about apple pie at the chief's house.

The Major

Billy was washing the hose wagon when he called to no one in particular, "Hey, the Major'll be coming soon!" It was 10:00 a.m., the time for him to make his appearance. Every morning, except Sunday, he would come walking down Cambridge Street on his way to the S & S Delicatessen for his morning cup of coffee.

We never really knew with absolute certainty, but by the almost marching like stride he used to walk, it seemed obvious that he had been in some branch of the military. He was an elegant dresser with the bearing of a true gentleman. I judged him to be in his late seventies. We all called him "the Major."

We had a large thermometer on the frame of the apparatus door that said *Drink Coke* or something similar. We had noticed that our tin soldier never failed to check the temperature. He never broke his stride when one of the guys beat a marching cadence on the apparatus door. If the traffic was heavy, his feet would keep perfect time as he waited patiently for Lenny the cop to give him the signal that it was safe to cross. He would then adjust his step with a jumping half step and march across the intersection.

One freezing morning we had the doors closed against the chilling wind blowing down Cambridge Street. Right on schedule at 10:00 a.m. down the street came our one man military detachment. He was dressed well for a cold winter day, complete with a warm muffler about his neck and galoshes on his feet. It was obvious that someone dressed him with loving care. One of the lads went outside and held a cigarette lighter to the thermometer and ran the temperature up to eighty six degrees. We all watched the Major's reaction. His nose was inches away from the numbers on the thermometer and he stared in disbelief at the instrument. Slowly he shook his head from side to side, and then, never looking in our direction, he started to undress. First it was the fluffy muffler, then the camel hair coat, then the wool sweater.

Now it was a serious question as to just how far he would go. Lenny the cop and four or five people were staring at him. How would we stop him? Our little joke had backfired on us. Finally the lieutenant said, "OK, boys, enough is enough!" He went out and told the gentleman that the thermometer was broken. Our friend said that it was OK and he was too warm anyway.

I felt guilty then, and I still feel guilty now that I had anything to do with making fun of this gentleman. Perhaps writing about it will make others more sensitive about people who are a little different, who may—for whatever reason—march to a different drummer and hear a different tune.

Barrel Factory Fire

For some reason Saturday was an action day, and this particular Saturday was no exception. Tom, our resident retired firefighter, saw the smoke from his chair in the second floor loafing room. He yelled, "Oh boy, look at *that*!" I was washing the hose wagon in preparation for Saturday afternoon inspection. Now I looked. A large black cloud of smoke was rising rapidly into the clear blue sky. The lieutenant was heading to the phone to check things out when the box started striking. Immediately we started to get into our gear because that smoke was close. The gongs were tapping out Cambridge and Willow Streets. The lieutenant had pulled the hook and the siren above the door was wailing. Jimmy Nugget was in the market across the street picking up groceries for lunch. When he heard the melodic wail he ran out of the market and dodged the traffic to get back to us. He was driving the wagon and we would go nowhere until he returned. It was my turn riding the rear step. I was hooking on my spanner belt as we crossed the threshold and holding onto the bar with my chin. The pump stopped at the box located two blocks away. People were standing out on Cambridge Street excitedly pointing down Willow Street. At the foot of the street was a large wooden barrel factory—it was totally involved in fire. You could feel the heat from half a block away. We dropped two big lines from the wagon. As the hose played out on the street I stepped to the far side of the rear step

—36—

to avoid being hit by the couplings. The wind was rushing by my ears as it was being drawn into the raging fire. A free burning fire such as this makes a fearful roar. Radiant heat was rapidly spreading the fire. People were evacuating their homes and pulling tables, chairs, washing machines and various religious statues with them. Fortunately the wind was blowing directly away from us and we could see. On the other side, leeward, the wind was pushing the fire up the street. Most of this factory was in the city of Somerville. They were having their hands full and had struck three alarms already. When the Cambridge chief arrived he immediately struck two alarms. The great danger in this type of fire is the very real possibility of a conflagration. The wind was picking up and large pieces of burning wood were being carried a great distance from the fire. Separate fires were starting on roofs three blocks from the main fire. As we were running the lines into the deluge gun on the wagon, people were screaming on the street. Panic was setting in. Flames were rising hundreds of feet into the air. Not only was the factory involved, we also had houses on boths sides of Willow Street burning. The heat now had us crouching down behind the canvas of the wagon. We were yelling to the pump operator to charge both lines into the gun. The paint on the hood of the wagon was blistering. The windshield was also cracking. There was a real possibility that we would not be able to hold our position. If the water didn't start soon we would be running with the other people.

As I looked back up Willow Street I saw a Cambridge chief calmly directing a Boston engine company into position. He stood there, tall and in command, as he gave orders. Generals do not run. Now the lines were starting to sputter to life. First rusty water, then a solid five hundred gallons a minute were arcing toward the spreading flames. The thick black smoke was rising rapidly into the sky and the crackling rumble of the flames overwhelmed other sounds. The Boston company was now looking for help in getting a big line up on the roof of a still uninvolved building. Cambridge Ladder 2 had a stick to the roof. Another guy relieved me on the gun and I was ordered to assist the Boston company. Using Ladder 2's stick we reached the third story roof. It was quite a view. I could see three buildings of the barrel factory complex burning, plus at least a couple of three deckers on the leeward side. The heat up there was horrific. We used a chimney as a heat wave break and I pulled the winter ear flaps inside my helmet down in an effort to save my ears from burning. Using hose ropes we tied the pipe to a roof vent to relieve the back pressure. The roof was flat and felt solid underfoot. Now I could hear it. At first it sounded like a low rumble and steadily increased in crescendo. Soon it was a roar. The lieutenant of Engine 26 said, "Come on boys, it's time to get the fuck off this roof!" Unknown to us at the time, fifty five gallon drums of flammable fluid were stored in the front section of the building that we were on. Fire had spread into the first floor. The ensuing explosion knocked us off our feet and a gigantic ball of flame swirled into the air. Heavy fire was now boiling out of the roof skylight. One of the Boston boys had broken his arm. The second explosion lifted the roof up. Now the smoke and heat descended on us. It was stifling and breathing was becoming a serious problem. I could feel the panic building in my chest. Visibility was now zero. The lieutenant was yelling, "Grab belts! Grab belts!" which meant to take hold of the guy in front of you. We were crouching low as we made our way back toward the ladder. Were we going in the right direction? The member with the broken arm was behind me. He was hanging on to my belt with his good hand. Another series of explosions shook the roof. They were not as strong as the previous ones. We passed a skylight and through the smoke I could see the rolling orange flame below.

The lieutenant had found the ladder. Everything was by feel.

When he climbed on the stick I could hear the ladder hit the building. Now we had another problem. Flame had blown out the windows directly below the ladder. We were cut off. The four of us crowded at the parapet and waved our helmets. I sat on the roof with my right hand on the ladder and started saying the Hail Mary. It's a strange feeling knowing that you are going to die. I was afraid. The brothers below knew our plight and were directing lines to knock the fire back into the building, but the heat and smoke were too much. I could feel myself getting weak and sleepy. The jake in front of me was also collapsing. The fire had been darkened down and we could pass the windows, and somehow, one by one, we climbed down the ladder. The lieutenant assisted the lad with the broken arm to an ambulance parked up the street that transported the injured jake to the hospital. I made my way back to the rear step of Engine 5 and sat down. My legs felt like rubber. Someone gave me an oxygen mask and the O2 helped. Today, looking back, I can't understand how the hell I could sit there and enjoy a cigarette after inhaling green tar smoke from the roof! The multiple alarm units were working now and good progress was being made. We were relieved at the fire.

That night Peggy and I had a PTA meeting at Michael's grammar school. I really didn't feel like going but Peggy said it was important. When we returned home I remember Peggy saying, "Gee, Hon, I heard on the radio that Somerville had a bad fire."

"Ya, they did," I replied. "I was there." After finishing my Hail Mary, I drifted off to sleep.

A Firefighter's Dilemma

Back in the good old days of long work shifts, it was sometimes hard for a firefighter to keep a decent home life, especially in the early days. You would go to work and be on duty for twenty four hours. You were granted a supper hour each tour and these were assigned according to seniority. A guy with little time on the job would get the last choice of supper hours. This made it very difficult for a wife to plan dinner for her firefighter. Or anything else.

There were times, of course, when he would arrive home for a little lunch and have a little of something else in mind. Invariably the kids would be home. Dad would sit at the kitchen table and give a special wink to his bride. Reaching into his trouser pocket he would pull out a half dollar coin. "What's playing at the Strand this afternoon, Cathy?"

"Gee, Dad we saw that picture last Saturday."

"OK, Cathy, my love, what's on at the Capital?"

"Gee, Dad that's Tom Mix and the Texas Rangers and they say its great!"

"OK then! Take your brother and go to the Capital."

"Gee, Dad we want to see Tom Mix but it's a double feature and we saw the second show."

Dad's eyes were now on the kitchen clock. "How about you taking your brother out for an ice cream cone?"

"Gee, Dad, that would be swell. Will you and mom take a walk with us?"

"You know, kids, we would, but I have to get back to the station and there won't be time. You kids go along and I'll see you when I get home."

"Gee, Mom, you can come along for an ice cream, huh?"

"You kids run along and enjoy," Mom replies.

After hugs and kisses off they go. Dad now gives his bride a coy smile and moves tactfully towards the bedroom. Just as Cathy comes back and says, "Gee, Dad it's starting to rain and I have homework to do. Maybe it would be better if I did the homework now and go to the show Saturday, OK!"

Have A Cigar

It had been snowing all night. When I reported to duty at Engine 5 in Inman Square, the first order of business was to shovel the front of the station. The night crew had already been at it, but their concentration was only the front of the apparatus doors. The captain was sitting at the desk reading his paper. When we started to sneak upstairs for a cup of coffee after putting our turnout gear on the rig, he bellowed out, "Come on, boys! Get out there and start shoveling!" Engine 5 was located at a very busy intersection. Just up the street from us was the Cambridge City Hospital. It was a freezing morning and my nose was running like an open faucet. Workers were making their way to their jobs.

As I leaned on my shovel, I commented to Billy McCabe that it was a shame we couldn't coax a city plow to give us a hand. Then I remembered there was a box of cigars up in Lieutenant Lively's room and he no longer smoked. Billy agreed that there was no harm and we could give the plow driver a fistful. Up I went and retrieved the cigars. Billy then stood out in the snow waving the bait. Soon a gigantic snowplow pulled in and went to work. The captain stood at the window watching the scene unfold with an approving look on his face. Back and forth the plow moved and soon all the snow was neatly piled in front of the house. It was a work of art. With smiling faces we gave the driver his fistful of cigars. He tipped his hat and away he drove.

I got a bucket of sand from the back room and completed the job. No one would take a nasty fall in front of our station.

I was up on the second floor mopping when I heard the plow again. Looking out the window I couldn't believe my eyes. The plow was pushing all the snow back in front of the station doors. How bizarre! The driver had the window open and was yelling, "You God dammed firemen!" or words to that effect. Billy and I slid the pole just as the captain was running out the door. The driver was telling the boss that he and the rest of us were a bunch of cheap bastards. The guy next to the driver was doubling over in laughter.

The plow operator was now out of the truck, face to face with the captain. He was spitting on the captain's glasses as he spoke. The boss was asking what the hell he was so upset about and telling him that if he didn't stop spitting on him he would arrange for him to take a nap on the snow. Riley the cop was now on hand and was asking what the hell was going on. The driver saw the cop, jumped in the cab and after a parting word about exactly what he thought of firemen, drove the plow down Cambridge Street, grinding his gears as he went.

We told the captain that all we did was give the guy a fistful of cigars. He then asked where we obtained said cigars. Billy and I looked at each and decided to come clean. We told the captain that the cigars had reposed on the lieutenant's bureau and he did not smoke. Our captain now asked us if we knew how long the cigars had been hanging around the station. "No, Captain," we responded in unison.

"Well, boys I gave those cigars to Lieutenant Lively as a gift...*about five years ago!*"

Billy's face was a little pale; so was mine. As we shoveled snow for the rest of the day we agreed that first puff must have blown that poor snowplow driver's socks off his feet.

A Christmas Fire

Christmas is always a busy time of the year for almost everyone and our house was no exception. At this time, 1956, Michael was still our only child, but he kept us plenty busy. I guess he was entering what is known as "the terrible twos". Somewhere along the line Peggy would ask me how I was working for the holidays. The department was as fair as possible regarding which group would be on duty. As a rule holidays were given off on a rotating basis. This year would be my turn to be on duty for Christmas Eve. Peggy never appreciated my working Christmas Eve; there were so many thing to do. We were having Peg's mother and father over for dinner and there was cooking to be done on top of the usual last minute gift purchases and present wrapping. Peg would take care of what she could and I would take care of getting the food.

    The early part of the tour was peaceful. I had the seven to nine p.m. watch and different neighbors dropped by to wish us a Merry Christmas. The district chief dropped in about eight and had a cup of coffee. It was just a little past eight when the box came in. It was a run for us. The chief and his aide hit the pole and were on their way. I was driving the hose wagon and could hear the radio. Engine 3 was going off with heavy smoke showing from the third floor windows of a taxpayer—dwellings over stores. The fire was on Cambridge Street and we were heading straight at it. We laid a line and were ordered to reduce to inch and a half. Engine 3 was advancing a line in through the front door and we would back them up.

The smoke inside was tough enough to cut your heart out, and this was still the time when protective masks were not commonly worn. Engine 3 had made it to the second floor landing and were stopped dead. I could hear action on the roof. Ladder 2 was opening up. When the roof was opened, it made a big difference. Visibility improved a bit, but the intensity of the fire increased due to more air being drawn into the fire from below. Engine 3 continued up the stairs to the third floor and we went to work on the second floor. Down the hall toward the rear the fire was roaring. Tongues of flame were lapping out the transom over a door and rolling down the hallway toward the front stairs. Somewhere someone was hitting fire because the smoke was down to the floor again. I put my face close to the linoleum on the floor but still there was no air. I again felt the awful sensation of someone holding me by the throat and squeezing. Up on the pipe the lieutenant was yelling above the roaring flames, "Back out! Back out!" This was fine with me; I had just about reached the point of not being able to take anymore. I had an awful ringing in my ears and voices were starting to sound dull and hollow. Engine 3 was not faring much better; they were also backing out. A voice from below us was yelling, "Engine Five and Three, get out! The roof is coming in!" From the outside I could see why we were ordered out. Flame was showing fifty feet through the roof.

We were now ordered to the rear of the building. The smoke was so heavy in the rear that we had difficulty finding our way down the alley. Using the rear fire escape, we were able to advance the line to the second floor and operated on heavy fire coming from the windows.

When the smoke lifted a bit we could see that it was a bedroom. Dragging the line over a bed I felt what at first I thought was a doll. It was no doll. It was the burnt body of a three year old girl. She looked like a little rag doll. Fishcakes found another body—a five year old boy—on the floor near the hallway. We had been so close and could not make it. Body bags were called for and members of the Rescue Company removed the victims.

Other companies were now getting a hand on the fire. It had started on the second floor in the vicinity of the rear stairs. After the fire was out we were held with Engine 3 and Ladder 2 until the detail companies showed up. I sat on the rear step of Five's wagon talking to Fishcakes. He was upset about finding the kids. Someone, probably a neighbor, had given us cups of coffee. Down the street we could hear people singing Christmas carols. Later I walked down the steaming dark hall. There was ice on the linoleum and it cracked under my boots. On the third floor landing I saw what to me looked like a glob of plastic on the wall. Taking it down and looking closely at it I knew what it was. A smoke detector. I held it in my gloved hand and noted that there was no battery in it. Later we learned that someone had removed the battery and put it into a toy.

It was 2:00 a.m. when we left the scene. After the wagon was re-packed and the guys had turned in I sat and looked out at the square. From the loafing room window I could see the twinkling colored lights in a tall Christmas tree that the city had put up in the square. It was Christmas morning.

Voting

Like many cities Cambridge uses various fire stations for polls on election day. At Engine 5's house we had collapsible wooden booths stored in the cellar. About three days before the election the group working would dig them out of their musty resting places and give them a wash down. The process of getting them up to the apparatus floor was accomplished differently each time. Due to their weight and bulk many backs fell victim in the struggle to properly place them.

On the day of the election we moved the pump and hose wagon to an adjoining bay. The election workers were always early and efficiently assumed their assigned stations. The precinct director was there and would oversee the entire operation. At the stroke of 7:00 a.m. the polls opened. Folks on their way to work at the local factories in the area were waiting at the door.

It was a long day for the poll workers. We would maintain the watch desk and stay out of the way as much as possible. When the polls finally closed, the fun began. Now it was time to count the votes. Two elderly election department workers would sit across the table from each other. The goal was to tally the total vote less any spoiled ballots; this figure should match the figure that showed in the glass window of the ballot box. It never did, of course. And this particular year, at midnight it was still not even close.

Billy Mac was sitting at the patrol desk reading the *Record American* that Top Shelf Sullivan had brought in from the S&S Restaurant. What we wanted to do was call it a night. Perhaps it was due to the hour or perhaps the devil made us do it, but Billy would ask me how much two and half hose we carried on the pump. The poll worker would be droning "sixty four, sixty five" and I would yell out "forty eight" and the counter would continue "forty nine, fifty."

The precinct warden did not appreciate our humor and we were warned to stop confusing the counters. The problem was that they were not organized when they started. Most of these poll workers were senior citizens whose normal bedtime was 9:00 p.m. They were just plain tired. At about 2:00 a.m. the precinct warden said, "Wrap it up!" and they strapped up the ballot box and took the ballots to a local school to be tabulated later. Cambridge is one of the few communities in the country to use an election process called "proportional representation" and the final results would take some time.

In any event, the election count at the firehouse was done until next time. Now we could get back to business.

Sunday Mass

It was a hot day in the middle of August. Usually when I worked Saturday night I was able to get out of the station a little ahead of schedule because Bob Harris would come in a little early. He was riding the rear step and was my relief.

It was handy living down the street from the station. I could walk to work and Peggy could use the car. This particular Sunday was different, however, and I was late getting home; we'd had a fire during the night and we did not get back to quarters until 6:30 a.m. Then we had to load the hose and check all the equipment.

Our normal Sunday routine was for Peggy to go to church first and I would stay home with Michael. Michael was our first son, and he was a screamer. He was having a tough time getting used to formula. While Peg was gone I walked around the house with Michael up on my shoulder, trying to calm him down so he wouldn't wake up the neighborhood. Finally Peggy came home and out the door I ran for the next Mass. There was no time to change out of my uniform.

The church was fairly crowded. I could smell the odor immediately. It was like something had died close by—like under my pew. When I returned to my pew after Communion, the strange odor was still there. However, all the people who had been sitting near me were gone! Where the heck did they go? I wondered. This was strange. The area for about fifteen feet on all sides of me was void of people. Then I saw her. She was an elderly lady and she was giving me a very dirty, very uncharitable look. The people weren't there, but the smell sure was.

Usually after Communion, the priest would sit for a few moments of quiet reflection. Not this time. The fragrance hung in the air like a black vine. It was powerful enough to remove varnish. The good father charged off the altar. You never saw anyone make such a hasty exit.

On the way out of church the mystery was solved. A friend of mine told me about the large glob of a white substance perched on my right shoulder. When I reached the car I took off the offending shirt and put it in the trunk. Peggy and I had a good laugh and she just shook her head, saying over and over, "Only you...only you!"

Peggy is gone now and Michael is a fire captain. Time can bend our back and slow our pace but as long as there are memories...We are forever young.

Golden Memories

Peg and I had been back home from our honeymoon for only a week. This was a period of adjustment. Even though we had known each other for a couple of years, the adjustment was still there—personal habits, schedules, preferences had to be negotiated, compromises had to be reached, and, of course, there were small arguments over things that are difficult to remember the next day. We were living in a three room apartment on the third floor of a building on Inman Street, just off Inman Square. It was very handy for me; I fell out of bed and was in the firehouse. It was also handy for Peggy since the bus stop was just down the street in Inman Square. On hot nights during the next summer, I would persuade the lieutenant to use our drill time to lay an inch an and a half line. We'd use the line to cool down the slate roof where we lived so Peggy could get the baby to sleep. The hot sun would beat down on the slate roof all day and the apartment would be hot all night.

We didn't have much but we were happy. The apartment was small and we couldn't squeeze a lot of furniture in there anyway, but I do remember that we needed a small table to put next to the bed. After talking it over, however, we decided to wait until we had the cash to buy one.

Vincent's Market was next to the station. One day I was in the market buying vegetables for the noon meal. Vinny was just finishing unpacking a two section wooden orange crate. To me the crate looked like a fine candidate for a small table next to the bed. We would be able to put the phone on it and perhaps a small lamp. Vincent said to take it, so home the orange crate went. I disguised its real purpose—its crateness—with a tablecloth. When Peg arrived home I proudly showed her my accomplishment—a night stand. She stood there, staring at the table/crate, and finally said, "I can't believe that you did that." I assured her that I, indeed, had come up with this ingenious idea and was very proud. She just shook her head from side to side.

A few weeks later we had some friends over to see our new home and I proudly lifted the table cloth and displayed my Yankee ingenuity. Peg's face turned first red, then yellow, and finally a mote gray. If looks could kill I was a goner. Even years later when I would reminisce about it she would still glare at me. If things had gone a little differently, who knows...maybe today it would be **Connie's Crate & Barrel Company!**

I suppose that being married to firefighter had its moments. When the phone rang in the middle of the night ordering me to respond to a fire, I am sure Peggy wished I had selected some other trade. Many times she would make plans to go somewhere only to discover that I was scheduled to work. I can honestly say that she would seldom complain. With a shrug of her shoulders she would say, "There'll be other times, Hon." One morning when she arrived at work her fellow office workers said that they were surprised to see her there. News of a major fire in Cambridge had been all over the radio—and I was on the list of men injured. Until now I never thought of how the ride in the subway and bus must have been for her. She had no way of knowing just how badly I had been injured.

We were married on February 22, 1954. Our first son, Michael, was born on December 2, 1954. A few folks did a little counting on their fingers. Peggy would get a big kick out of their concern. When asked directly she would only smile, and I would kid her that even if we didn't have much money on our honeymoon we did have some fun. Mike had a rough case of colic and was a screamer. I had to go out and get him goat's milk. We took him to a doctor who said that he was confused whether he should prescribe for us or for Mike. As I said in an earlier piece, Mike's a fire captain now. Of course, there are those who work with him who swear that he is still belly aching.

The second born was Cornelius, junior. As a youngster he was a quiet, laid back kid. He excelled in running—especially when I called him in for a bath. We almost lost him when he was five. One day he ran out between two parked cars and was almost killed. He had a severe head injury and was unconscious for two days. He also is now a firefighter.

With a gang of boys haircuts were an expensive matter. Someone gave me an old used barber chair. It had been down a cellar in East Boston and I guess it had fleas. I purchased a hair clipper and comb set. A small section of the cellar was set up for hair cutting. I improved the lighting in the area and covered the floor. After supper on Saturday night the little shop opened. All was ready—the old sheet to keep the hair off their clothes, a table to lay out my tools, and a small radio that would play as I clipped away. Sometimes a little too much was taken off one side and then the other side would be cut to even things up. One time I finished up with Neal and sent him upstairs to Peg for a bath and from the cellar I heard her scream, "What have you done to our son?" I guess as a barber I had a ways to go. Another time Michael moved and a small piece of his ear came off. The little shop closed and we spent the evening at the hospital. Peg never suggested that if I got tired of being a firefighter I could always become a barber.

Getting out to work at night was sometimes hectic. One time as I was rushing around looking for my uniform hat, Peggy was trying to tell me that our two year old son, Michael, was sick with the croup. She asked me if she should give him a little whiskey to break up the congestion. It was supposed to be an old Irish remedy. As I was searching under the kids' beds for the hat I yelled, "Half a finger."

I had just settled down at work and looking at a nice cup of coffee when the lieutenant yelled up the pole hole that I had a call. It was Peg: "Connie," she said, her voice full of concern, "Michael's acting real funny. When I look at his eyes, one's going one way while the other's headed in the opposite direction." I told her that help was on the way.

The Rescue lost no time getting to the house. When I arrived at the hospital, poor Peg was sitting in the waiting room sobbing. There we sat, waiting and crying, when the doctor came out and informed us that our son was drunk. He asked me how much whiskey the child had. Poor Peg had misunderstood me and given Mike three fingers. That was enough to knock down a horse! We were given the duty of walking our giggling son up and down the hospital corridor. At any minute I thought we would be arrested for child abuse.

The boys slept on the third floor and I was always nervous about getting out in case of fire. On the kitchen wall I installed a big red fire bell someone had give me. There was only one exit from the third floor so I installed a knotted rope and shackled it to the front bedroom floor. Without prior notice I would conduct a fire drill. When then bell sounded all the boys would run up stairs and exit from the window then slide down the rope to safety. Peggy would not allow the girls to participate. Mrs. Gillian, the lady next door to us, would see the boys coming down the rope and say, "There goes the O'Brien Fire Brigade again." When the drill was over I would rate them on performance and timing. Peggy just shook her head.

When I was ready to start haircuts I would call upstairs. The boys wasted no time running to the third floor and sliding down the rope. Mrs. Gillian would say, "Gee that's funny; I didn't hear the bell." For Easter, however, Peg insisted that I take the boys to Tony's Barber Shop down the street. This hurt my feelings a bit; I really thought that I was doing pretty well with the clippers. One day I was in the barber shop getting a hair cut when I spotted two old barber chairs in the back room. I just had to find out what they did with retired barber chairs, so I asked Tony. He stopped cutting my hair, swung the chair around so that he could look me square in the eye and said in a convincing voice, "They sell them to cheap bastards like you." The remainder of the haircut was conducted in utter silence. Poor Tony felt bad about what he said and apologized. I assured him that he was only telling it as it was.

Stephen was the next to come along. He loved ice hockey and used this talent to put himself through college on scholarships. Next came Timothy; he broke tradition and became a police officer. He now can be seen riding his police Harley Davidson around the streets of Cambridge. Eugene arrived on Christmas morning 1962. The world has not been the same since. He too was a great hockey player and after high school became an electrician.

Just when we were all geared up for boys, along came our first daughter, Eileen. After surviving living among five brothers, she graduated from college and became a paralegal. Jennifer was the last arrive. After college she became an actress and school teacher. It's not surprising that she followed an acting career—after all, my father used to call me a bad actor.

Looking back down the road now that they have all gone their separate ways, it is a bit lonely. Peggy is gone now and that part of my life is like a precious happy interlude. We cannot recapture yesterday, but in the silence of reflection, the golden memories will always be there...And there is tomorrow.

A Toy Factory

The fire was already a general alarm when Cambridge Engine 5 was dispatched. The city of Medford is located about eight miles northeast of Cambridge. Somerville had already responded and had three engine companies working at the fire. When Five left quarters they could see the heavy plume of black smoke looming up before them. It was just past noon on Saturday when Fire Alarm dispatched them by phone to the fire; they told them that it was a toy factory complex.

The traffic was light and they no trouble finding the fire because you could see it for miles away. A chief from the Medford Fire Department was at the Powder House Square traffic rotary to direct them. They were instructed to lay a big line down the railroad tracks to the rear south side of the complex. The pump was located at a hydrant on Warren Street. As the line played out from the rear of the hose wagon, Captain Ellis and Joe Mahoney stood on the rear step. Another chief was waiting for them and he ordered them to advance the line into the second floor of a two story wing of the main fire building that faced onto Boston Avenue. He also told them there was no fire in this building and Five's line would only be used as a cover. There was no smoke whatsoever on the second floor so visibility was good. Captain Ellis noticed that this floor was loaded with cardboard cartons. He also noted that the section was sprinklered. They dragged the dry line down the eight foot center aisle two hundred feet to where the fire door separated the two sections. Windows lined both sides of the storage room but were difficult to access due to way the cartons were stacked. Captain Ellis sent one man back with orders to charge the line. A deep low rumble started to shake the building. Looking up at the ceiling, Captain Ellis saw swirling black smoke pushing from around the large closed metal fire door and moving quickly across the ceiling. The air was still and he felt a kind of dryness in his mouth. None of the men were wearing masks. His next command was *"Run!"* In seconds the smoke was near the floor. He could feel the heat building up behind them as they ran. Using the stacked cartons as a guide they all bolted for the door. Joe Mahoney was the first to reach the stairs and tumbled down, then Bob. The captain was still about twenty feet from the stairs when it blew. He was picked up by the flaming concussion and slammed against the wall near the stairs. Thick black smoke was now pushing out the door where Joe and Bob lay in the ground. Joe yelled, "Where's the Captain?" Holding his breath against the searing hot smoke he made his way back to top of the stairs. Captain Ellis was crawling toward him in a dazed condition. His helmet was gone and he was stunned. The entire wing was now completely involved in fire. Heavy flame was showing from all the blown out second floor windows.

Medical help was at their side in moments. All three members were taken to the hospital. The captain was horribly burnt. The explosion had blown his helmet off and he was burnt about the face and hands. Joe and Bob received second degree burns of the face and ears.

Meanwhile, the fire was now a surround and drown job—that is, only an exterior attack is allowed. Joe and Bob were released from the hospital but the captain was transferred to the Massachusetts General Hospital Burns Center. His hands received the worst of it—third degree burns. He was scheduled to take a written examination for deputy chief in two weeks. This, of course, was out of the question. When I went to the hospital to visit him he never mentioned the exam. I knew he was that type. He accepted his fate as a man.

Now as my mind surveys the years, certain men stand far out or maybe a little higher than the rest. Fire Captain Walter Ellis is one of them. He retired holding the rank he held that day of the fire. Today his son, Walter Ellis Jr., is Assistant Chief of the Cambridge Fire Department. The branch has not fallen far from the tree.

DUFF SPRINGS

Mystic Avenue is a wide, potholed thoroughfare in Medford adjacent to the Mystic River. The street is home to a wide range of garages, factories, metal working shops, and junkyards. One of the larger garages on Mystic Avenue was named Duff Springs. They specialized in repairing large trucks and buses. The City of Cambridge subcontracted with Duff Springs to install heavy duty springs on the fire apparatus. One day I was detailed to the repair garage and we took a ladder truck over to have work done.

It was a beautiful spring day. They had a large sign planted in the small bit of grass in front of the building. There wasn't much room for any type of grass in front of the garage. As a matter of fact, that sign stood on the only patch of grass on Mystic Avenue.

As Billy and I stood there waiting for the work to be completed, I commented that this would make a fine setting for a family vacation. Billy's eyebrows scrunched up and his mouth dropped open as he looked back at me. I continued, "This place has everything, Billy—even a nice view of the Mystic River!" In the background we could see Kelly's Junkyard. Dark plumes of acrid smoke gently rose from some old wreck they were burning. The downtown Boston skyline was radiantly silhouetted against a clear blue sky. It was a picture post card setting. Then the idea came to me. From then on whenever the kids asked me where we were going on vacation, I would proudly answer, "Duff Springs."

That night I tried to get Peggy to be an accomplice in my plan. We would take all the kids over there and pose for some pictures. The kids could wear their bathing suits. The scenes would show Peg and I stretched out on folding lounge chairs and holding cold drinks. The kids would be playing in the little patch of grass. In the background would be the sign, **DUFF SPRINGS**. We would have post cards made and sign the post card "Greetings from Duff Springs" and mail them to all our friends.

I was engrossed in describing this evolving plan to Peggy. Of course, there would be a danger. We would have to watch out for the large dump trucks pulling in and out of the garage. "And, of course, Peg," I said, "we'll probably have to buy the kids new clothes 'cause you'll never get the grease out of the ones they wear to Duff Springs!" I paused and looked to Peggy for approval. Peggy just stared at me with her dark brown eyes, slowly shaking her head from side to side. Then she spoke: "When we are committed to the nutty ward for observation who would take the kids down to the Charles River in the evening to watch the sail boats?"

I then turned my face away from her and, scratching the side of my face said, "You know, Peg, you've got something there."

So much for Duff Springs.

COTT BOTTLING PLANT

The people across the street were looking up Beacon Street and pointing, then I saw Lennie Payton, the police officer who was directing traffic in Inman Square, running across the street pointing up Beacon Street and looking up at us. He was excited and yelling, "Look, look!" Just as Billy McCabe went outside and looked up Beacon Street, the phone rang down at the patrol desk. Lieutenant Galvin pressed the still button and yelled up the pole hole, "We're going' out!" Billy's eyes were wide with amazement as he told us that the entire sky up Beacon Street was black.

I was riding the back step of the hose wagon, and when we made the turn I could see what everyone was getting excited about. Indeed the sky was jet black. A strange, deep chill came down my back; it had happened before…it would happen again. I suppose it was fear, the kind a soldier feels just before he goes into combat or an athlete feels just before the game starts.

This fire was not in Cambridge but just across the line in Somerville on Washington Street. It was the Cott Bottling Complex. Three buildings were already fully involved when we arrived. The Cott complex consisted of nine or ten wood frame, one to three story factory buildings. The wind being generated by the fire was laying the flames against the uninvolved structures. The wind was blowing out of the southwest, a normal direction during the summer months.

Charlie made a hydrant on Washington Street across from the fire and we would be on the windward side. The lieutenant was indicating that he wanted me to drop two big lines. The hose wagon pulled into a large parking lot and we ran both lines into the deck gun.

It's strange how thinking about a job jolts back memories. I still remember a man walking across the parking lot and the rush of wind being sucked into the flame pulled his hat off his head and it sailed into the inferno. The neighborhood around the plant consisted of three story, wood frame tenements. Downwind from us the fire had already crossed the tracks and involved a few houses. This fire had all the makings of a full-fledged conflagration. The wind was right, the fire had a hell of a start, and there was plenty to burn in front of it.

The heat was becoming unbearable, even with our helmets reversed and with turnout coats and gloves. It was becoming increasingly obvious that we could not hold our position. I pulled the canvas deck cover up so we could hide behind it, but it wasn't much help. Superheated air can pin you down and instantly burn any exposed flesh. The windshield of the hose wagon was cracking and we were breathing through our noses to avoid inhaling the superheated air. Another company operated a line on us and we were able to hold our position. Boy, that water felt good.

This fire was heading straight for Union Square and gaining momentum fast. There were no natural firebreaks such as parks or wide streets to impede its progress. The method of attack in this type of advanced fire is to get on all sides of it and wet down where it is going then pinch it off before it gets there. This requires a heavy concentration of water application and manpower. A command chief will waste no time in summoning the necessary help to accomplish control. Somerville Chief of Department O'Hara, an experienced and determined firefighter, had no intentions of allowing this to happen. Mutual aid apparatus from Cambridge, Boston, Everett, Medford, and Arlington were dispatched without delay.

We were relieved on the gun and ordered to advance a big hand line to protect exposures. As we advanced the line between a one story garage and a building, bodies began falling down in front of us. They were Boston jakes who had just been washed off the roof of the garage. One guy landed directly in front of me. There were four of them. They had fallen about fifteen feet. Somewhere on the other side of the fire a ladder pipe went into operation and had swept them away. All four were seriously injured. The operators of the ladder pipe never saw the Boston crew. Ambulances were waiting in the parking lot and the injured firefighters were transported to local hospitals. Later I heard that the injuries ranged from broken bones to internal injuries. Between the smoke, water spray, low visibility, and the personnel confusion that these types of fire sometimes created, accidents such as this were more apt to happen. Also, back in those days radio communication was unheard of. It would be impossible to know where everyone was working.

A bit down the alley we bumped into a district chief who ordered us to advance our line inside a two and a half story dwelling to check fire that had extended into the cockloft. We reduced to inch and a half and dragged the line to the attic. The chief had a ladder company in there with us and they started to open up the ceiling. We found fire in the walls and ceilings. An exposure such as this will ignite quickly. Another company had a line below us and had their hands full. Soon it was obvious to us that our position was becoming untenable and we would be forced to retreat. Now the boys below us were yelling for us to back out.

With some degree of difficulty we were able to bull the

charged line down the stairs over debris that had fallen from the ceiling. Even as things inside the building were really coming apart, the outside also had a surprise waiting for us. While we were within the building the adjacent structures had become involved. We were now in the middle of a raging inferno. The other engine company had moved up the alley and was pinned down by the almost unbearable heat. They were yelling for a cover line so they could make it to the street. Just about then someone opened up with a deck gun and the cool water began cascading on us. It sure felt good. We all made it out to the street and were able to drag our line with us.

The fire now had gained full conflagration proportions. Men were dragging lines to feed water into appliances that had been repositioned. At this time we were playing catch-up. The fire had extended beyond the line that had been established to control it. Chief O'Hara quickly recognized this danger and had sounded the general alarm. This would bring additional help from adjoining cities and towns.

Ladder pipes and deluge guns were put into operation. A major fire such as this will also create another serious problem—water. This element becomes an absolute necessity. Many older cities and towns, still to this day, do not have adequate water resources. Old four and six inch mains just cannot move sufficient water to control a wind driven conflagration. This fire was now generating its own wind and involving buildings at will. Structures well in front and to the sides, not directly touched by the flame, were beginning to smoke due to the fact that radiant heat will extend out 360 degrees in all directions, even against the wind.

After a tough fight, sufficient streams were put into operation and the fire was brought under control. The fire had just about wiped the plant out. The total count was about twenty fire-fighters injured, some of them quite seriously. We were relieved from the fire and sent to a cover assignment. There was a sub shop across the square and I was assigned the task of making a list of who wanted what. When I went to pay the bill the owner said in broken English, "No charge! No charge! Fire was heading for me! God bless you firemen." I thanked him and left the store thinking that people's gratitude made it all worthwhile.

Dimmick Street

Charlie was looking at my car motor and telling me the reason the engine was bucking was the cheap gas I was using when I heard the long ring of the still bell. We had been dispatched by phone to respond to Somerville box 236 for a fire on Dimmick Street. Due to our location right on the line we would beat the first due Somerville companies by a mile.

I was riding the rear step of the hose wagon. When we turned right onto Calvin Street I could see the smoke. This is a heavily congested tenement area where the three deckers are leaning on each other. The pump pulled over and I laid a two and a half line from the wagon. Heavy fire was now showing from the rear first floor windows of a three decker. Overlapping fire was now involving the rear porches. In many cases range oil was illegally stored on these porches, and on occasion these drums would explode, showering the area with burning oil. We took the big line in the side yard and the lieutenant ordered it to be operated on the rear porches in order to control the spread of fire. This type of fire will easily spread to adjacent porches and we could have a conflagration on our hands. Somerville was now on the scene and going to work. They were advancing a line in the front door to cover the stairs. The distance between the houses in the alley was only about seven feet. A woman was hanging out the window of the adjacent house and yelling that there was an invalid man in the first floor rear bedroom. This room was heavily involved. We used the big line against the ceiling to kill the heavy fire. The woman was still screaming that the man was definitely in there. I jumped up on the fence and dove into the room. Billy and some other guy were covering me with the line. The man was there all right. The bed was next to the window and I had landed squarely on top of his chest. Naturally we didn't have masks at that time. It was impossible to breathe. I had to get out of there fast! With my arms I reached under the man and pulled up. There he was, nose to nose with me and quite dead. His face was burnt black and the skin was hanging off. Leaving the man behind, I dove out the window. The truth of the matter was that he scared the shit out of me.

The fire went to two alarms. When it was knocked down the body was removed from the room. There was no one else in the house. I assisted in placing the man into a body bag. We had just lowered the bag out the window when a chief called to me. He said that the man's arm had fallen off and told me to find it. This I did. It was still there in the bedclothes.

We were dismissed from the fire and returned to quarters. After we loaded dry hose on the wagon I told the lieutenant that I was going down stairs to check the donkey heater. I descended the stairs to the cellar and vomited into the coal pile. I didn't want to let on that I was sick. I deposited the evidence into the furnace. This was my very first experience with death by fire. I guess the first is the hardest. I took a lot of kidding about that fire and diving out the window. Even to write about it some forty years later gives me a strange sorrowful feeling. As it turned out, when I was eating supper one night not long after the fire, my mother asked me about the incident. She said that the man who had died in the fire was a friend of hers and a fellow member of the Irish American Club. He was recuperating from a serious operation and his wife had just gone to the store to do some shopping. She also said that he was a heavy cigar smoker and wondered if that had any thing to do with the fire. The piece of steak and the gravy on the potatoes on my plate seemed to transform a bit. My reply as I left the table was, "Gee, Mom, that dinner tastes great, but I'm not too hungry right now. Maybe I'll heat it up later."

An Armory Fire

Deputy Chief O'Hara's aide was on vacation. He called Engine 5 and asked me if I would drive him for two weeks while Elliot was away. I had never served as a chief's aide and thought the experience could be interesting. Division 1 relieved at Engine 9 quarters on Lexington Ave. When I arrived there on Monday evening the Division 1 car was there. Bobby Long said it had been quiet all the day and he wished us a slow night. As we pulled away from Engine 9 Chief O'Hara reminded me that we did not put out fires, so speed was not a serious consideration. He continued: "As long as I get to the fire in one piece, that'll be fine, Connie." We stopped off at headquarters and I checked the box in the deputy's office to see if there was any correspondence to be delivered to the division. There were papers to be distributed.

The first stop was Engine 5, which was fortunate since I wanted to pick up my pillow and night hitch. We had a cup of coffee with the boys. Chief O'Hara had been the captain of Engine 5 and he liked to re-visit the station. We finished the rounds around 7:30 p.m. and were on Memorial Drive, along the Charles River, when the tone came on the radio and then the dispatcher's voice announced, "Striking box three four one one for a building fire at the corner of Massachusetts Avenue and Albany Street." When the radio signal had been completed, Fire Alarm called us. "Fire Alarm calling C Two."

"C Two," Chief O'Hara acknowledged.

"We now are receiving calls for a fire in the armory on Mass. Ave."

The chief said that he had the report. Engine 2 and Ladder 3 are quartered about three blocks away on Mass. Ave. Ladder 3 reported off at the box with heavy smoke showing from the Albany Street side. When we turned onto River Street, Engine 6 was right in front of us and making plenty of noise. We were about a block away when Ladder 3 called, "On the orders of Lieutenant Randall, box three four one one is a working fire." This was a second class, four story, building that was occupied and still used as an armory. Smoke and fire were showing from the third floor windows. We reported "off at the fire". On the report of a working fire, Fire Alarm will automatically dispatch an additional engine company to the scene. Engine 2, who had entered the front door on the Massachusetts Avenue side, called the chief on the fire channel and reported that they were on the third floor and advancing a big line. Ladder 3 had the stick to the roof on the Albany Street side. Captain Randall called the chief and reported that fire was blowing out the rear windows on the third floor and they were in the process of opening up the roof.

Chief O'Hara was standing in front of the armory. Using the portable radio he called Fre Alarm: "On the orders of C Two, strike a second alarm—box three four one one." He didn't have to be in the building. The reports that he had received from the companies clearly indicated that extra help would be needed. The second alarm would bring him an additional two engines and one ladder company.

Engine 6 was ordered to advance a big line up the side fire escape to the third floor. Engine 2 was now reporting that the fire apparently involved two rooms on the third floor. They further reported that they had water on the fire. Engine 5 was

—71—

ordered to run a line to back up Engine 2. Ladder 1 checked for extension of the fire on floor number four. They were backed up by Engine 7. This was still the time when the Rescue Company had the only mask protection; they had all service type masks. The chief ordered them to conduct search and rescue with a ladder company to make sure there were no occupants. The search was negative—everyone had escaped from the building. A lieutenant who worked in the armory reported to the chief that small arms ammunition was stored in a closet on the third floor. The chief advised all companies to be aware of the possibility of exploding shells.

The second alarm chief was at the scene and took command of the operations at the rear of the building. Chief O'Hara told me to get up to Engine 2 and report to him on how they were doing. There was a fair amount of water coming down the wide stairs. Visibility was good until I reached the third floor. Now it was time to get on my knees and follow the line to where it was operating. I could feel a railing on my left. The smoke conditions would cut your heart out and visibility was zero. The line was leading me straight ahead. Suddenly I was falling. Then nothing. I felt a heavy weight on my chest and breathing was difficult. It was like having the wind knocked out of you. I just couldn't breathe. Hot water was hitting me on the face and neck. I couldn't feel my arms or legs. The speaker of the portable was next to my cheek and pressing into my skin. They tell me that I was making funny noises into the radio. Maybe I was singing, I don't know. I do know that I wanted to get the hell out of there. The tangle of debris was smoldering and the smoke was suffocating. Bob Gillette from Engine 6 found me. He had to crawl in from the first floor hallway. I had fallen fifteen feet. No one told me that the floor had ended and the railing had burned away! I don't know why I wasn't killed.

Getting me out was a bit of a problem. When Bob found me

I was jammed between heavy pieces of debris. All that was clear was my head. The wind was knocked out of me and breathing was extremely difficult. The Rescue used a jack to get me out. After all the smoke had cleared I ended up with a broken back plus a few cuts and bruises. My stay in the Cambridge City Hospital lasted about three weeks. It was the middle of summer and as hot as hell in there. No air conditioning in those days. They got me a couple of fans and that helped a little. The big problem was that the dammed traction kept me from moving and was uncom-fortable as hell. Peg was there by my side much of the time. I often wonder if she had second thoughts about marrying a "fireman". I am sure it wasn't easy for her. The ladies behind the shield are a special breed. They are truly as brave as any firefighter that I have ever known.

A few days after this fire they had a three bagger in an apartment building on Mass. Ave. Some rescues were made over ladders. They removed one man who was badly burnt on the chest, face and legs. Somehow he ended up in a room down the hall from me. The poor guy moaned and moaned all night. I was having trouble sleeping due to the traction and heat, but my problems were minuscule compared to his. Later I heard that the fire had started in his apartment. He was a cigar smoker and had fallen asleep. He woke up and found the bed on fire. A neighbor heard him yelling and found him down the hallway. The fire consumed a couple of rooms on the fourth floor before they could knock it down. The third day the odor coming from the hall was tough. Human tissue was decaying. A priest who was a friend of mine came to see me. The poor guy was sitting there beside me getting ill by the minute. When I finally told him about the fellow down the hall, he said that he would pray for him. The burn victim died on the fifth day and, I guess, they had to fumigate the room.

The boys showed up a couple of times and wanted to push

my bed down the block to the Polish American Club with me in it. Cooler heads prevailed and they were asked to leave. I was never again asked to drive a chief. When Elliot returned from vacation he kidded me about not making it in the big time. Driving a chief was not my cup of tea. I was happy riding the rear step of the hose wagon with my back to the wind.

Officer Mulligan

As I stood by the radiator on the apparatus floor looking out the window at the cold winter night I saw him. He was across the street, standing at the police box. In those days the police officers didn't have radios; they would check in with the station by signal box.

Now he was crossing the street and headed for the station. The temperature outside was holding at twelve degrees above zero with a sharp wind blowing out of the northeast. I had the ten to midnight watch. Remaining seated at the desk was out of the question due to the cold wind blowing under the apparatus doors. The only salvation was to wrap yourself around the radiator.

Officer Mulligan entered the firehouse and pressed himself against the radiator with me. "Gee, Connie, it's *cold* tonight!" he said. I agreed and told him that there was hot coffee upstairs. It was 11:00 p.m. and the second half would relieve him at midnight. He thanked me for the coffee offer but said he would hold out for midnight.

Usually when the phone rings at this time of night it's a run, but this time it was the fire dispatcher looking for Officer Mulligan. He took the call and then told me that he had to go across the street to the "flat iron block", a triangular block with stores on the first floor. There was a rat stuck behind a radiator and he was to inform the rodent that it could not warm itself there.

The last that I saw of Pat he was making his way across Cambridge Street to solve the problem of the rat. Top Shelf Sullivan came in with the *Record American* newspaper and I was sitting at the patrol desk reading when I heard the shot. There was no mistaking the sound—it was a pistol report.

The phone rang and we were dispatched to the flat iron block for a cellar fire. That was where Mulligan was. Box forty one was being struck with a full assignment. Large clouds of steam were rolling out the cellar windows. Steam is often mistaken for smoke. Companies were told to hold up in laying lines; an investigation was under way to determine the source of the steam.

When the steam cleared the story unfolded. Cambridge Police Officer Patrick Mulligan had attempted to solve the rat problem by using his thirty eight to shoot the visitor behind the radiator. The bullet went through the floor and hit the steam furnace in the cellar causing it to explode. When the chief in charge asked Officer Mulligan why he followed this course of action, Pat replied that he had tried everything from cheese to chopping but the damned rat would not leave. The chief just stood there and shook his head.

About a week later my six gun buddy came into quarters. The subject of the rat reared its ugly head. I had no intention of trapping him but I did ask him if he hit the rat. "No, Connie, I didn't," he replied, "but I think the steam got him."

About a month later Officer Mulligan rang the emergency bell outside the firehouse. He reported that there was a barrel burning in front of the bank. It was four o'clock in the morning. "Why the hell didn't you just piss on it?" the lieutenant asked. Officer Mulligan replied that he hadn't been drinking much water. We all walked back to the station shaking our heads.

Holes in My Lids

The two to four watch in the afternoon was hard, to say the least. The chances were pretty good that you would be alone. The lieutenant would be up in the company office and the other guys would be either studying for exams or examining their mattresses. Fighting sleep at the patrol desk was not easy. When you were on floor patrol you stayed right there. If you had to leave the desk area you would shake the sliding pole and ask one of the guys upstairs to answer to phone.

This particular summer afternoon I was really sleepy. Our new baby Michael was colicy and we were having a hard time with him. He was our first and we hadn't quite got the parenting knack yet. We took him to see the doctor who looked at us and said that he was trying to decide if he should prescribe something for the baby or for us. Sitting at the desk with my uniform hat tilted over my eyes I fell asleep. When the company journal slammed down on the desk, however, I was fully awake—and there he was. The division chief holding the book with both hands down on the desk.

I leaped out of the chair and in my most enthusiastic voice said, "Good afternoon, Deputy."

He did not reply. Instead he spoke in a raised voice, "Hoseman O'Brien, were you asleep?"

Thinking nimbly on my feet I replied, "Chief, remember that fire we had at Carlson's Lumberyard? Well, flying embers burnt my eyes and I was checking my eyelids for holes."

His hands relaxed on the journal and he had a peculiar look on his face, as if he could not believe what he had just heard. I didn't believe what I'd just heard either!

Now he spoke; "Get the officer down here."

"Yes, sir," I replied. Using the still bell I rang twice. Lieutenant Galvin walked down the stairs and stood before the deputy. I stood at attention next to the patrol desk. The hose wagon had been involved in an accident the previous week and the deputy wanted to see the damage. They both went to the rear of the apparatus floor for the inspection; I couldn't hear the conversation. Oh boy, I thought, you've done it now. Engine 9 here I come. As they walked back towards the desk the chief was staring at me. He had a reputation of being an excellent firefighter and a fair man. As we both stood there the chief picked up the phone. This is it, I thought. He's going to make arrangements for my transfer. The chief asked Fire Alarm to connect him to the mechanical shop. Oh boy! I was to be assigned to the mechanical division, probably as a grease monkey or blowing up tires without an air pump. Woe is me! When he finished talking to them he told the lieutenant to send the wagon to the shop tomorrow for repairs. Turning to me he said in a very authoritative voice, "Hoseman O'Brien is having a problem with his eyes, Lieutenant. If the condition does not improve we may have to move him to a station where there is less chance he will see smoke."

After the chief left the lieutenant asked me what that was all about. I replied, "Gee, Lute, maybe he thought I looked tired."

Until the day he chief retired he never forgot to ask me how my eyes were doing. I always replied, "Wide open, Chief! Wide open!"

A Boat Ride

We were sitting around the coffee table at Engine 5 waiting for the change of shifts when the discussion turned to fishing. Charlie said that he knew a guy who lived in Wellfleet down on the Outer Cape who owned a big boat. After a few more fishing adventures were fabricated and swapped, we told Charlie to contact his pal and we would make plans for a fishing expedition. About two weeks later Charlie informed us that plans were shaping up. It was late August and saltwater fishing should be fine Our host down the Cape was a fellow who had recently retired from the *Boston Globe*. When Dave retired from the newspaper he took to the good life. He married for the third time; his new bride seemed to have plenty of money. Dave's new bride gave him a thirty five foot Chris-Craft power boat for a wedding present. He was all set.

Although they were well off, they led a strange life. Shortly after they were married she told him they were through. He was a great guy when he was sober, but those times were few and far between. Anyhow, we arrived at his Cape Cod combination honeymoon/separation cottage about eight in the morning and there was a problem right off the bat. Dave was nowhere in sight. The house was a long, one story ranch. The garden to the right was beautifully kept. The one to the left was so overgrown with weeds that it looked like an abandoned lot in Cambridge!

Finally Dave responded to our gentle tapping. "Why the hell don't ya knock? There ain't no one here 'cept the dog and me." The dog was barking—I think at him. He looked like he'd been on a week long bender. He also looked like a square meal would kill him. We were invited into his domicile. Pizza boxes littered the floor, a half eaten sub lay on the coffee table, and the dog was still barking at our host. And, of course, Dave was anxious to show us the rest of the house. This cottage was split into two sections—hers and his. He said that she was out of town and he knew how to get into her half. By this time I was ready to go home. He insisted and we were ushered into her side. Naturally, it was the complete opposite of his. Soft pastel colors blended with white and gold trimmed furniture. The feminine touch was everywhere. Fresh flowers, probably cut from the garden on the right side of the house, were tastefully arranged in a vase on the living room coffee table. Dave explained that he and his bride were not hitting it off. He said that she had her lifestyle and he had his; thus the house was split in half.

It was now fishing time. The rods and bait were loaded aboard and off we roared. It was around 10:00 a.m. when we finally got under way. If I had known what we were in for, we would have stayed at home. The weather was fine with partly cloudy skies. Not one of us had bothered to check the weather. We all assumed that details such as this would be taken care of by our fearless captain. We were horribly mistaken. All Dave was worried about was the beer supply. Charlie, Russ and I liked to have a beer or two, but we all knew that drinking on a boat can be dangerous.

Late in the afternoon the dark clouds started to roll in. It was only 3:30 so this seemed strange. I don't know how far we were out but on a clear day I bet we could've seen the coast of Portugal. Dave and the other guys were finished fishing. We had done OK. Between us we had three big buckets of cod, haddock, and flounder. It was now clearly time to head for home. As the captain turned the boat around, lightning flashed in the western sky.

Dave told me that he had set a course and all that I had to do was steer west northwest at 160 degrees. This would take us to the mouth of the North River. Hmmmm. Now darkness enveloped us and the waves were getting larger. The bow was headed directly into the tempest. Charlie and Russ were now beside me and both wanted to know if it was time to sing "Nearer My God To Thee". I was too busy trying to keep the heading Dave gave me. Finally I yelled to Charlie, "Get that imbecile up here and check things out!" When they got Dave to the bridge he didn't have a leg under him and the pitching deck had nothing to do with it. He was loaded. Apparently he had found a cache of beer he'd forgotten about. With bloodshot eyes and slurred speech he said that I was doing fine, just fine. This vessel had a main and an fuel auxiliary tank. The gauge on the instrument panel was in the red zone so Russ checked the main tank. Now it was really raining and the wind was picking up. I had some experience with boating but I was lost in this kind of situation. Even with the windshield wipers going it was impossible to see past the bow. Charlie was twirling the knobs on the radio and I thought that I could hear Latin American music.

About fifteen minutes had passed since the good captain had set the course. Charlie stumbled forward and now was telling me that he could hear, over the roaring wind, water smashing against rocks. I thought, That must be the dark blob that I saw on the radar screen. Hmmmmm. Captain Dave was now beside me and blaming me for the nasty turn of events, and as if we did not have enough troubles, the motor was now sputtering. Russ had his mouth hanging open as he pointed over the starboard bow. There it was, a big lighthouse directly in front of us and getting bigger with each surge of the sea. The good captain saw it too and was now giving more orders than Admiral Halsey in the Pacific. He was spinning the wheel just like he knew what to do. For a brief moment we were all proud of him. With a wave of his hand he ordered the switch to cut the auxiliary tank be thrown and this was done. Now the captain's mouth was open. The auxiliary tank was only a quarter full. "Nearer My God To Thee". Later we learned that Dave had no money and was too proud to ask us.

Things could not get much worse, so they started to get better. The depth indicator said that we had fifty or so feet of water under us. Charlie had made some coffee in the galley and we were urging Dave to drink some. The mouth of the North River came into view and our sea adventure was almost over. The sky had cleared and there was going to be a beautiful sunset.

On the way home we stopped at a Howard Johnson's in Kingston for a cup of coffee. We sat silently at the counter when Charlie said, "Close only counts in horseshoes."

"Even so, Charlie," I responded, "that was close enough."

We never saw Dave again. Maybe he went to sea and found a new home.

The Harvard Lampoon

Saturday nights could be a challenge. Usually we'd have a good number of false alarms. In some cases the same box would be pulled three times in a row at about thirty minutes intervals. When it was busy, we would just go from one box to another. To the kids pulling the boxes it was fun, but to us it was a potentially deadly game. I have seen firefighters lose their lives directly due to false alarms. People would sit on the wooden steps of their houses, see us racing around, and know perfectly well that their kids were pulling the boxes. Occasionally we would catch one and the mother would swear the culprit was with her. I honestly couldn't understand their mentality. Things usually quieted down about midnight. Any boxes after that would be either a die hard box puller or an actual fire.

We were having a cup of coffee at twelve fifteen when the box came in for a fire in the Harvard Lampoon's building. This is a four-story brick and wood, oddly shaped building; from the outside it resembles a miniature castle. It is part of the Harvard University complex of buildings and stands out prominently at the junction of Mount Auburn and Plympton Streets. It was constructed of brick and wood and has been there for many years. There are narrow slit windows at the second floor level, hardly of any value in firefighting. The Harvard Lampoon is an undergraduate humor club that specializes in publishing parodies of legitimate newspapers and magazines.

It was a midtown box and we were slated to respond on the

second alarm. The first arriving company, Engine 1, reported heavy smoke showing and ordered a working fire. As always, the heart beats faster when the magic words "working fire" are spoken. It did not take the working chief too much time to order a second alarm. The fire had a good head start. The second floor was used as a lounge and had a gigantic fireplace at one end with a beautiful hand carved wood facade. Apparently, the fire had started behind the fireplace, probably due to the roaring fire they'd had earlier. We responded on the second alarm and reported to the command chief on Bow Street. We were ordered to advance a big line over a thirty five foot ladder and get into the second floor via the slit windows. This was no easy task. First, there was little room to squeeze through the slit. Secondly, we were not sure where the floor was. It is vital to check the location of the floor—firefighters have been killed entering windows and falling into the cellar.

The ladder company had broken the glass in the windows and heavy black smoke was pouring out. When I reached the window sill, the opening looked even smaller. With a mask on viability is zero. You could find yourself perched on the top of a bookcase and the first step could be quite alarming. Bracing my foot against the right beam of the ladder, I was just about able to get into the building. Fishcakes was right behind me. It was black as midnight. To my right, I could see an orange glow. We pulled in enough line to work with. From the sounds of things crashing down on the floor, we figured we had to be in a good-size room. I could feel tables and chairs. The floor felt solid. The room was not particularly hot. Fishcakes was in the window opening and pulling in hose. Now I could hear other streams operating, and the lieutenant was with us now. Crawling on the floor, I advanced the line toward the orange glow in front of me. I could hear someone yelling, "It's gonna blow!" Just then our line sprang to life—we had water. A sheet of flame erupted in front of us and sped over our heads. The superheated air descended on us like a crushing weight and drove us to the floor. Lieutenant Galvin yelled for me to open the line and direct it over our heads in a fog pattern. Hot scalding water cascaded down on top of us. Our fog stream was being superheated and had become boiling water.

Conditions were becoming worse. It was time to get the hell out of the Lampoon Castle. When we got back to the window a serious problem waited for us. Getting out the narrow opening. Visibility was zero due to the thick acrid smoke. The regulator on my demand type Scott was clicking fast, indicating that my air supply was depleting which would cut down on escape time. The lieutenant was pushing Fishcakes through the slit window, but his air cylinder was caught in the opening. Breathing was getting difficult and I thought we might be running out of air. The window was clear and I was being boosted out. Lieutenant Galvin yelled to me to work the air tank out first. Somehow I got out onto the ladder. Fishcakes was down and safe. Now the fire was really pushing. Flame was not far away. It was making up to blow. I frantically pulled the line out, giving the lieutenant a little more room. He had one booted leg out and on the ladder when a shuddering explosion actually blew the lieutenant out the window and into my arms. At times like this, firefighters are blessed with a super strength from somewhere and I was able to steady the lieutenant onto the ladder. With the exception of having the hell scared out of us we were OK.

The fire went to three alarms and there was extensive damage done to the interior. Earlier in the evening, the lower lounge had been used for what was then called "a smoker", but would now be called a drinking bash. There is a massive fireplace in the lower lounge and apparently, a cozy fire was provided. When the fire was under control, we reentered the structure. Now we could see the reason for the flashover.

Heavy varnished oak paneling had covered the walls. The fire, after starting in the rear of the fireplace, had run the walls and entered the second floor dining area.

In the process of overhauling, it became necessary to get behind the fireplace. Someone got the less than brilliant idea of tilting the mass of bricks out to wash down the rear wall. Lieutenant Galvin, three other guys and I were told to steady the tilting mass of bricks. The only trouble was that the massive pile of bricks was now tilting at us. The angle of tilt had passed the balance stage and now was about to crush us. One by one, the boys were bailing out. Each time one left the weight became more oppressive. The lieutenant looked at me and I stared back at him. His eyes were saying that it was time to leave. There was no holding it now; it was coming down on us. We were dead in the center and there was no time to run. My arms were being pushed back into my body. Looking up I now could see the fancy brick façade over the mantel leaning toward us. To this day, I can honestly say that I don't know how we managed to do it, but simultaneously we both dove into the firebox and the dammed thing fell around us. There was now a complete blackout created of dust, smoke and debris. In the middle of all this chaos, out of the firebox we emerged.

If it were not for the Lampoon Castle's heavy timber construction, we all would have undoubtedly ended up in the cellar—and that wouldn't have been funny at all!

Hot Pipes

Having a large family meant sometimes it was necessary to bring a little extra money into the house. I had done some plumbing in the past, but I was by no means a qualified plumber. One day I was sitting at the floor patrol desk when a fellow came in and asked if any of the firefighters might be available to give him a hand with a plumbing job. I couldn't believe my luck! "I'm your man, mister."

Eddie and I hit it off immediately. He had just received his master plumber's license and was looking for a part time helper. His work for the most part consisted of jobbing; we would make alterations on old work and install new bathroom and kitchen plumbing. I had been working for him on my days off for about three months when we started a job in Somerville installing a new kitchen sink on the second floor of a wooden three story dwelling. Normally, a job like this would be a piece of cake. As it turned out, however, this cake never left the oven.

We removed the old sink without incident, then Eddie made a list of the stock necessary to complete the job. He told me that he wanted to make the trip to the supply house because he wanted to look at another job. Before he left he showed me what I was to do while he was gone. It was simple. All I had to do was hold the propane torch against the soil pipe hub until the old lead melted. Sounded simple enough. Although the pipe was positioned in close to the varnished wooden wainscoting, Eddie said that if I was careful this would be no problem.

As he went down the rear stairs he yelled back that he would pick up some coffee and doughnuts. Everything was set. Everything was under control. Carefully I started the heavy duty, 40 lb. propane torch, making sure that the supply tank was far enough away from where I was working. No one was home in the apartment. There I was holding the torch against the hub as I was told to do. Five minutes passed and there was no sign of melting lead. Hmmm? Then I heard a gentle knock on the kitchen door to the back stairs. I opened the door and discovered a young lady with a baby. She politely asked me if there was supposed to be smoke in her apartment on the third floor. As I looked over her shoulder I could see smoke was also in the hall. I raced up the back stairs and into her kitchen where I found heavy smoke coming from the wall right above where I was working. Call the fire department! Call the police! Call the pope! The dammed place is on fire.

I ran back down the stairs two at a time and asked the woman if anyone else was in the building. With her bright eyes gleaming panic, she told me that her invalid grandfather was asleep in her third floor apartment. A phone was on the kitchen wall of the apartment where I was working. I told her to call the Somerville Fire Department and report the fire and then get out of the building. Woe is me!

Running back up the stairs and into the kitchen I could see fire in the walls with heavy smoke layering four feet from the floor. I found grandpop in the front bedroom, peacefully sleeping. I shook him gently and announced the fact that the house was on fire. "Who the hell are you?" he asked and rolled over to return to sleep. Now the smoke was lower and we had little time to become acquainted. Grabbing him under the armpits I succeeded in getting him on the floor. He still wanted to know who I was and what this was all about. Then he became aware of the smoke. "We'd better call the fire department and get everyone out," he said to me. I didn't say that that was what I was trying to do! When we reached the front of the house he saw his granddaughter and the baby.

The engines arrived at the scene, and it didn't take long for the district chief to call a working fire. I wondered if I would still have a job when this was all over. Greeting the lieutenant on the front porch I told him where the fire was. My plans of assisting the boys in extinguishing the flames were doused when I was pushed aside and told to stay out of the way. Proper lines were run and ventilation was made. After considerable damage the fire was contained and extinguished—with no help from me.

Eddie had completed his business and saw the plume of smoke as he approached the scene. "Ah no, it...it can't be," he murmured under his breath as he drew near. "O God, it is!" he screamed as he approached me.

"Gee, Eddie, it was an accident, you see." My plea was falling on deaf ears. The look that he gave me made me look at him through my shoelaces.

The fire was out and now someone with a clipboard wanted to know what happened. Tactfully I explained the circumstances and how remorseful I was while Eddie was wringing his hands and repeating "Ah shit! Ah shit!" over and over. I could tell by his body English that my plumbing career was drawing to a close. One of the men rolling hose saw me talking to the man with the clipboard and said, "Hey, aren't you on Engine Five?" I felt like Peter in the Garden of Gethsemane when he denied Christ. I was tempted to deny that I was a firefighter, but I decided, what the hell and answered "Yes." The guy with the clipboard did not bat an eye. Eddie provided the rest of the necessary information.

When we did get up to the floor where the fire started, I saw that the apartment was not damaged very much. They had opened the walls to get at the fire but other than that it was OK. Our tools were where I left them. The third floor was another matter. Now the owner of the house was there and shaking his head. The kitchen wall and part of the roof were severely damaged. Later, as we sat in the truck eating our doughnuts and drinking coffee, I asked Eddie if I was still employed as a plumber's assistant. He looked at me and said, "Sure, Connie. I started a few fires myself."

Some years later I was talking to the man who had the clipboard that day. He was now a district chief. When I asked him, he told me that yes, he had heard me acknowledge the fact that I was a firefighter. "Well, how come you never mentioned me in the reports?" I asked.

"We all make mistakes, brother," he said. "We all make mistakes."

Sledding, Anyone?

The kids really wanted to go sledding. They'd been begging. It had been snowing for most of the night and the temperature was hovering around twenty degrees. I was due to go on duty at 6:00 p.m. Having a day off had been good. A few things needed to be done around the house. Peggy was after me to fix a leak in the drainpipe under the kitchen sink and I had managed to put it off for a week or so, but now she was getting angry. We were living in a big two and a half story house in North Cambridge which we'd purchased on a wing and a prayer. Mike was eight, Neal six, Stephen was four. And the remainder were too young to go sledding.

Finally I relented and told Mike to dig the old sled out of the garage. Peggy said she would not have anything to do with the venture—she was smart. Off we went, along with a couple of neighborhood boys who heard about the trip. Soon we arrived with our wagon load and a sled tied on the roof. Kingsley Park was not very crowded and conditions looked perfect. The boys selected a hill that was not too steep and down they went. They were having a great time. I had my eyes on the clock because I had to get home for supper before I went in to work. It was getting late and we'd started to walk back in the direction of the wagon when Mike said, "Gee, Dad, why don't you take a ride down the hill by yourself?" With all my boys cheering me on, I got on the sled and away I went. As I picked up speed, I thought, This is great! My weight carried the sled much further down the hill. Oh boy! I realized I was heading directly at the lake. Not to worry, it'll stop—and stop it did. The front of the sled broke through the ice on the walkway. It abruptly stopped at least twenty feet from the water. All is well? Not quite. The sled stopped but I had kept going. The head of a nail was sticking up right where I was sitting. It tore a nice hunk of flesh out of my ass.

The boys came running down the hill yelling, "Are you OK, Dad?" I was all right but my rear end was bleeding like a stuck pig. We made it home and I showed Peggy my wound. She just stood there and laughed, then said, "Hon, I do believe you'll need a few stitches." There was no time for that; I was due in work. With the tears of laughter rolling down her cheeks she did her best to stem he flow of blood and apply a dressing. I ate my supper quickly and headed off to the firehouse.

After roll call I was sitting at the table in the loafing room enjoying a hot cup of coffee when I noticed the lieutenant looking at me strangely. "What's the problem, Loo?" I asked.

"Connie, I would like to ask you a personal question," he responded.

"Ask away," I said.

"Are you having your period?"

"What do you mean, Lieutenant?"

"Well I noticed that the rear end of your pants has a rather suspicious bloodstain."

After showing him the wound he suggested that I seek medical attention. At the hospital I bared my butt to medical scrutiny as the engines waited in the parking lot. The doctor agreed that it was quite a tear and, using four stitches, he closed the gash. For an encore I was given a tetanus shot by a giggling nurse.

The sled stood by the rubbish barrels the following Friday

waiting for a ride to the dump. However, it disappeared before the rubbish was picked up. I do remember hoping that its new owner repaired it before sliding down a hill.

Mineral Spirits Fire

I stood there looking down at the tragic site. The kitchen floor at Engine 5 needed another coat of wax. It also needed to be stripped. Just a new coat of wax would not disguise this fact. As I stood there, contemplating my next move, Tom, a retired firefighter, was in the loafing room looking out the window. I happened to glance at him and saw that his mouth was hanging open. He was pointing a slightly shaking finger out of the window. "Wow, look at that!" he called. A great plume of jet black smoke was rising in the sky. The lieutenant down-stairs was shaking the sliding pole and telling us to look out the window. Then the desk phone started ringing. Lieutenant Galvin answered it and yelled up the pole that we were to cover Somerville Engine 3 on the second alarm in their city.

Now I could hear the factory horns sounding as I slid down the pole. These were located in Cambridge and Somerville and were used to sound a multiple alarm. Box 313 would be 1-2-3—1—1-2-3 blasts. I yelled to Tom to finish the floor and his reply was something like, "I washed my last floor in this place years ago, bucko. You do it when you come back."

I rode the rear step of the hose wagon as we sped up Springfield Street and I could see people standing on the sidewalk, pointing at the sky. In the distance great clouds of gray black smoke were rising rapidly upward, covering an extremely large area, and I wondered what the hell could be on fire. As we were backing into the Union Square firehouse, we could hear the station gongs sounding the third alarm. The phone at the vacant patrol desk was also ringing. Lieutenant Galvin answered it and was told to respond directly to the fire at the Mineral Spirits complex on Mystic Avenue.

A good portion of the Mystic River is a kind of extension of Boston Harbor that runs northwest. It is a deep water channel and its shores are lined with various types of commercial properties. Fuel oil barges and coal ships unloaded at the power generating plant nearby. The fire involved at least three large storage tanks at the Mineral Spirits Company's complex. This plant manufactured paint thinner and other highly flammable types of solvents and was located on the banks of the Mystic River. At least three or four additional tanks were seriously exposed. Great plumes of orange-black flame were shooting rapidly into a clear blue sky. The weather would not be a factor as the day was cool and clear. The wind direction, on the other hand, would be a serious factor as the flames were impinging on other exposed storage tanks.

As we responded down Mystic Avenue past the front of the complex, the heat wave almost took my breath away. I had the trap up on the rear of the hose wagon waiting for the pump to pick up a hydrant. The only problem was that there were only a few in the area and they were already in use. A chief officer from Somerville was on the street waving us down. He asked the lieutenant if our pump could draft, which, for the uninitiated, is raising water by using suction. We had a 1935 Seagrave 1000 gallon pumper which was in fair shape for a seventeen year old piece. City master mechanic Justin McCarthy had recently overhauled the pump and it was in good working condition. Lieutenant Galvin responded that we could draft. The chief jumped up on the side of the pump and directed us down Mystic Ave. where we stopped in front of a large chain link fence gate. We were about fifty yards away from the fire. We were also on the lee side of the fire so the heat and smoke were right in our faces.

The gate was locked with a chain. While we waited out on Mystic Avenue, a tractor trailer smashed through the gate and out onto the street. Parts of the gate went flying in every direction. We were able to position the pump close to the embankment. Fortunately, the tide was in; it would only be about an eight foot lift to draft water into the pump. We tied a controlling line to the soft suction in about four feet of salt water. I glanced to my right at the awesome spectacle in front of me and saw the flames actually lapping against one of the exposed storage tanks. Before the chief left us he told the lieutenant to run three big lines into our hose wagon deck gun and cool down the sides of the uninvolved tanks. He also said that if we weren't successful he would see all of us in hell!

With his words ringing in my ears I watched the pump operator squeeze the handle to the priming pump. The hard suctions with a strainer on the end were submerged and all was ready. As the priming pump whined and strained to draw a suction, I uttered a prayer. Leo McDonald was perhaps one of the best pump operators we had at Engine 5. First one line to the gun fluttered then filled with water, then the other two sprang to life. Now he advanced the throttle and a solid stream shot out of the two inch tip at eighty pounds nozzle pressure. The chief was standing near the broken gate and gave us a thumbs up. It was a proud moment.

Much of the stream was turning to steam before reaching the metal sides of the exposed tanks. The fire was awesome. It sounded like a thousand freight trains. Even the most experienced firefighter had that deep sick fear in the heart, the feeling that makes you want to run, but yet you stay because it's what you're paid to do. We now ran an inch and a half line with a fog stream to cool us down. Billy and I worked the deck gun back and forth on the side of the tank. We turned our helmets around to partly protect our faces. Without the hose playing cooling water on us we would never have been able to hold our position on the wagon deck. Later, we were told that the tank contained lacquer thinner. When I heard that piece of news my knees became a little weak.

Not long after we were in full operation a Boston engine company went to work about twenty five yards away from us. They also operated a gun on the same tank. We sat up there on the wagon working the gun for about one hour, then two Medford firefighters relieved us on the gun. Out on Mystic Avenue we located a Salvation Army truck and had a cold drink. The sides of the burning tanks were now collapsing inward. All the tanks were in a spill containment diked area that was full of burning fluids and water.

After we finished the drinks we were ordered to work on the Boston fireboat, Engine 47. They had us unloading five gallon cans of mechanical liquid foam from the below decks storage compartments. The tide was now going out and soon the fireboat was high and dry and lying in mud late in the afternoon. When we finished unloading the foam we helped set up for foam application. The lieutenant in charge of the fireboat was all upset because he lost the tide change and was high and dry. The main body of fire was now showing signs of darkening down. All of the diked areas were filled with foam. You could still see a small amount of fire around a shut-off valve. Two firefighters volunteered to get into a rowboat and cross about twenty five feet of foam to attempt to shut off the flow of liquid and extinguish the remaining fire with a foam line. As they moved across the foam covered surface there was a flash and the boat was engulfed in flame. The entire surface within the dike re-ignited. Other big lines with fog streams were in place to cover them and immediately went into operation. The boat was pulled back and amazingly the men, who never panicked, were not injured. It had been a real close call for them, one, I suspect, that will linger forever in their memories.

We were sitting on the rear step of the hose wagon when the chief from the Somerville Fire Department came over to us. He congratulated the company on playing water on the exposed tank. The tide was way out when we made up our lines. It was now 4:00 p.m. and we were dismissed from the fire. As I rode out of the yard on top of piles of dirty hose I remember thinking You won't see us in hell this time chief. Not this time.

Captain Foley's New Toy

The good news was out. Engine 3 was to get a brand new television set! All the groups had pitched in to raise money for the purchase. It had taken six months to put aside sufficient funds. At the time TV was just leaving its infancy. To the best of our knowledge it would be the first TV in any of the firehouses in the City of Cambridge. It was to be a real big thing. Plans were made. The area near the slop sink was selected to be the location. Captain Foley was afraid that if the TV were located on the second floor it might slow down response time. Yes, near the slop sink would be the best place.

The captain had arranged delivery on a day when he would be on duty and the big day had finally arrived. The TV was scheduled to be delivered around 10:00 a.m. When the division deputy picked up the morning reports, Captain Foley shared the good news with him. He also told the chief that he would be more than welcome to drop by any time to enjoy the set. There would be Saturday Night Fights and other TV spectaculars. The screen was to be a whopping twelve inches!

The housework was finished early in anticipation of the momentous event. Captain Foley was humming his favorite Irish ditty when the phone rang. It was the training division reminding him that the company was due at pump training at 10:00 a.m. The captain's face turned first to red, then to green. His gray head shook gently back and forth. He could not believe his ears. His voice stammered a noise that sounded like he was in pain. He now sat heavily down at the desk and we all thought he was about to cry. It would seem that after he left Engine 3 Division Chief Spencer had gone to the next station and set it up with training to give the good captain a jolt. "Do ya think it at all possible if we attended training laaaater in the week?" He was now assured that this would be fine. He hung up the phone and pulled a rather large and not too clean blue bandanna out of his pocket and blew his nose.

    I was upstairs mopping the hallway when the truck arrived. We all slid the pole to give assistance as necessary. There it was, in all its glory. The TV cabinet had a sort of mahogany finish that shined and glistened in the sun. It was a truly beautiful thing. Captain Foley was carefully removing the packing material. A table, specifically for the purpose, had been set up at the appointed spot. The captain was speaking: "Oh, boys, look at it! Ain't that the best?" Larry Rose had devised a clamp that would secure the TV to the table. The captain said that we could not be too careful. The guys from Ladder 2 would drop by when they got a chance and install a proper antenna on the roof. We all placed our chairs in front of the set and Captain Foley was about to plug it in when—"Striking box one nine nine one for a reported building fire at one five one Gore Street." This box is located four blocks away and away we went. There was no one at the box; there was no 151 Gore Street. The captain radioed Fire Alarm to check the call. Chief Spencer was now at the scene. It was a malicious false call.

    Years ago we did not have automatic doors at the firehouses. Sometimes you would go on a run in the winter and when you returned the apparatus floor would be ice cold and the radiators would be jumping off the wall and the coal furnace in the cellar would be doing a dance. The second floor would be a toasty one hundred degrees. The oil burner thermostat was located on the rear wall of the apparatus floor. As the driver made the turn to back the hose wagon in I jumped off the rear step. Then I saw it. A two wheeler, the kind a longshoreman would use to move freight. The captain also saw it and was now running into the station. The worst had happened. They had not only stolen the TV, but also the damn table it was on. We all just stood there. We had not been gone that long, but it had been long enough to complete the dastardly deed.

The captain just stood there, staring vacantly at the empty spot. At last he reached into his back pocket and out came his soiled blue bandanna. After giving his nose a good blow he slowly turned and walked up the stairs. His head was down and he really looked dejected.

The next day we were sitting at the rear of the engines having a cup of coffee when Larry said to the captain, "Well, Cap, at least we gained a two wheeler to put the ash barrels out." Captain Foley turned his head toward Larry but did not say a word...not a single word.

Jordan Marsh Warehouse

Sometimes in the profession of firefighting circumstances come together to form an extremely dangerous situation. The Jordan Marsh warehouse fire in East Cambridge during the summer of 1965 was a victim of circumstances.

Although it is no longer part of our regional retail landscape, in 1965 Jordan Marsh was perhaps the largest department store operation in New England. That summer had been very hot. New England was in a mid-summer drought. There had been no rain in the Cambridge area for weeks. To complicate things even further, the area near the Jordan Marsh warehouse had a severe water problem because the city had contracted to have the water mains cleaned and relined. At the time of the fire there were four inch surface mains in the vicinity of the warehouse. All engine companies were made aware of this water shortage. The warehouse was seven stories and measured four hundred by one hundred feet. It was sprinklered and had a standpipe system. There was a loading dock and receiving area at the rear. At the time of the fire approximately five trailer trucks were waiting to be unloaded. Exposure was not a serious problem. The building was surrounded on all sides by large parking lots.

Lieutenant Lynch sat at the patrol desk of Engine 7, located about a mile from the Jordan Marsh warehouse. He was waiting for the deputy to pick up the morning reports. His mind was going over the events of the coming day. This would be in-service inspection day. It would be a good opportunity to have the crew take a look at the area effected by the water main work. Engine 7 was not normally first due. Engine 3 and Ladder 2 were quartered about five blocks away on Cambridge Street. The lieutenant's train of thought was interrupted by the radio: "Striking box one seven three six for a reported building fire on Commercial Ave...Deputy, we are receiving calls for a fire in the Jordan Marsh warehouse." The chief acknowledged. Fire Alarm was now reminding all responding companies that there was a water problem in the area. As Engine 7 crossed the threshold onto the ramp they could see that jet black smoke was already showing over the buildings.

Engine 3 and Ladder 2, first due on the box, pulled out and turned left onto Cambridge Street and the sight that greeted them was enough to send a chill down their spine. They not only saw smoke but also fire in the sky. The fire had started on the top floor and was blowing out all the windows on the northeast side. Normally a fire in this building would not have gained such headway. The sprinkler system would have held it in check until the arrival of the department. However, due to the water main work, there was less water pressure.

Lieutenant Lynch had his company position at a surface hydrant on Commercial Avenue and connected two two and half inch lines into the sprinkler Siamese connection on the front of the building. When the pump connected to the water supply, they realized that there was very little pressure. Both lines were charged into the system and the compound gauge read zero. Engine 3 ran two big lines into their deck gun on the wagon and found that they had the same problem—no water. Upon arrival the deputy immediately ordered a second alarm followed by a request that a third alarm be sounded. He also ordered responding engine companies to take a water supply from the large diameter main on Cambridge Street.

The heavy fire was now blowing out the fifth and sixth floors half way across the parking lot on the northeast side of the building. Fortunately, the warehouse was a freestanding building so there was no exposure problem. Giant balls of searing flame were boiling over the heads of the men who were attempting to get into operation in the parking lot. The windshields of the apparatus were cracking. The paint was cracking on the engines. They said it sounded like a gigantic blow torch over their heads. Ladder 2 was attempting to get into position to use its ladder gun. The exposed parts of their bodies were burning. The windward side of the building was rapidly becoming untenable. A shallow creek ran at right angles to the warehouse on the windward side. The heat was now so intense that men were forced to slide down the embankment into the water to cool down. Mutual aid companies from Boston and Somerville were setting up drafting operations from the Charles River. Rescue Company members had used hacksaws and acetylene torches to cut the steel fence. Lines were laid into pumps near the fire building and their residual pressure was improving.

Engine 5 was ordered to advance a big line up the front stairs. Things weren't bad until they reached the fourth floor where a gigantic ball of flame met them. As they crouched against the cement stairs the bulk of the fire passed over their heads. There was simply no way to advance against such conditions. They retreated to the street.

Now the fire was being fed by the contents of the warehouse, many of which were highly combustible items. The fire was dropping down to involve the lower floors, possibly gaining quick access through the conveyer systems or elevator shafts with open freight doors.

When deluge units were finally placed into operation, the intense heat was turning the streams to steam and not reaching the fire. The fourth alarm had been sounded. All interior firefighting was stopped and the men were ordered out of the building. The crew of Engine 6 had entered through the loading dock in the rear of the building. They had advanced a line up the rear stairs and had reached the fifth floor. The scalding hot water boiling down the cement stairs was burning them. Boston Engine 4 was on the third floor backing them up. When the backdraft occurred, the lieutenant of Engine 6 was on the fourth floor landing. They were cut off. Holding the line over their heads, the men started down the stairs. Visibility was zero. Cascading hot water was steaming them alive. Boston Engine 4 fought their way upward and assisted Engine 6 back down through a tangle of hose lines and dense black smoke.

The fire had now dropped down to the second floor. Heavy fire was still blowing out of the parking lot side. Deck guns and ladder pipes were now in full operation and things were looking much better. After three hours of hard fighting, units were able to get back inside and attack the fire from within. Ladder pipes and deluge guns were shut down. Big lines were advanced into the building. The damage was substantial. Cardboard boxes were soaked with water and the contents completely ruined. The contents of each floor had to be overhauled, and a first alarm assignment remained at the scene for two days.

I don't recall ever hearing what actually started the fire. However, there were a few good reasons why this particular fire acted this way. First of all there was a shortage of water in the area. The upper floors of the warehouse were loaded with highly combustible stock. This fire would have been held in check if the sprinker had had proper pressure. Also, firefighters are quickly effected by dehydration. This can lead quickly to hyperthermia which can have fatal results.

The members working will always remember this fire. As for me, I was glad I was off duty that day and swimming at Walden Pond with my family. You can't make them all!

A Time to Study

He stood there in the snow. On the top of his bell uniform hat there were at least two inches of the fluffy white stuff. He didn't move; he just stood there looking directly at our house. His double-breasted uniform overcoat was buttoned to the top against the cold January wind. I knew what he was waiting for—a ride to work. Peggy was now beside me looking at him. "Connie, get him inside! He'll freeze to death." It was six thirty in the morning and normally I wouldn't leave the house until quarter of seven. I now opened the door and asked Jerry if he would like a cup of coffee while I finished dressing. He waved and said that he was fine and would wait outside. Jerry had about thirty years on the job. He had been assigned to various companies and was well liked. He did his job and only spoke when he had something to say.

After saying good-bye to Peg and the kids I said a silent prayer and turned the ignition key. Lo and behold the old Chevy cranked into life. I just never knew when the dammed thing would start. Jerry was assigned to Engine 8 and I would be going right by his station. As he wiped the water from his glasses he asked me how things were going at Engine 5. I told him that all was well. He then said, "Rumor has it that there'll be a lieutenant's exam next year." Turning his head sideways at me he continued, "Connie, I told you a long time ago you have to wait for the wave. Well, there's a wave coming and you have to be ready." What he meant was that at certain times a group of officers pack it in and retire. It would happen every six or seven years. This also meant that you didn't necessarily have to be a great student to get a job. "The wave is almost here! It's time to ride, Connie."

After dropping Jerry off at Engine 8 I continued on to work. Yes, there would be a wave. The only trouble was that with a big family it was very hard to find time for any studying. We had three little ones at the time, and Peg and I were out straight. The only quality time to study was in the afternoons at the firehouse. I had already taken one exam and didn't fare too well. I was what you call an *also ran*; I passed but not sufficiently high to get promoted. I do remember feeling a bit jealous of those who did well.

One night when Peg and I were sitting over a cup of coffee, she said that I should think seriously about getting promoted. After telling her what Jerry said, we decided that now was the time to plug. With the kids and my other responsibilities—at the time I was working two jobs—this would not be easy. However, studying exclusively in the firehouse was not an avenue of success. There are just too many interruptions. So we would have to create a study regimen at home, which is what we did.

For the better part of a year I studied hard. This was a real sacrifice for Peggy and the kids. The lieutenant's exam was scheduled for Saturday, August 8th. I had been at the books for about ten months. As the date gets close you start to think of all the areas you failed to cover. Math and spelling had caused me trouble the first time. Michael, my oldest son, was attending Saint Peter's Catholic Grammar School. One day I was talking to a nun at the school about the exam. She asked me to let her look at a copy of the Fire Manual. When she returned the book to me, all the tricky words were highlighted in yellow.

Through the grapevine I heard that Mr. Bloomburg had some "hot material" that I should be looking at. His office was located on Washington Street in downtown Boston. Mr. Bloomburg was a very well respected authority on civil service examinations. I paid him for some study material and was about to leave when he asked me to look at a math hydraulics book he'd just received that contained sample problems and answers to questions that could be asked on the test. I scanned the pages, knowing that my money was spent and all that I had left was subway fare home. Mr. Bloomburg seemed to read my mind: "Connie, that's a good book and you should have it." There was no way out. I bit the bullet and told him that my money was gone. I'll never forget the look on his face. He said, "Take the book! We can even up after you have been promoted."

The Saturday before the exam was as hot as it gets in August. As usual, Peg made me a lunch, gave me a kiss and off I was to go to the cooler climate of the Mystic Lakes where I would sit in a beach chair and study. On the front porch Michael, Neal, and Stephen were waiting for me. Michael was the first to speak. "Gee, Dad, all the kids have gone to the beach. Can we go too? Please, Dad." It was just too much for me. Re-entering the hallway I threw the books on top of the freezer and in a commanding voice said, "Enough is enough! Let's go to the beach."

Peggy was there behind me. She put her arms around my neck, looked me directly in the eye said and said, "No, I want you to go and study. I also want you to remember this moment before you start the exam." I did. When the marks came out I was in the top five. Needless to say I was elated.

During my career, many men have asked me how do you study for promotion. I would always tell them that there was no magic formula. The only secrets were sacrifice and study. Of course, it's always helpful to have a Peggy or a Mr. Bloomburg to be there for you. Incidentally, Mr. Bloomburg's book contained many of the hydraulic problems that appeared on the test. My promotion party was held above Engine 5. The evening of the party the florist delivered a dozen roses to my wife from the boys at Engine 5. The morning of the party I had given Peggy a single rose from me.

A Visit

When I read the notes the captain had left me, a smile curled my lips. We were to have visitors this evening. Since I'd been assigned as lieutenant of Engine 1, someone always seemed to be paying us a visit. The note stated that a group of medical students were scheduled to visit the Rescue unit and we were to answer any questions that they may have concerning engine company operations.

Engine 1 was my first permanent assignment as lieutenant in a company since being promoted. Prior to this I was a floating officer between Engine 4 and Engine 9. Floating was a real pain in the ass. You had two captains to deal with, two different crews, two different stations, and half the time I wasn't sure where I was supposed to be. Headquarters was a busy station. Engine 1, Ladder 1, the Rescue Company and the division chief ran out of there. Sometimes it was a real nut house. All night someone was moving. The busiest company was the Rescue. They took all box alarms and medical calls. It is strange but there was a waiting list to be assigned to the company.

When the Rescue returned from the run, I told Walter that he had company coming. He was not too happy: "Why the hell do they pick on our group! Why can't they leave us the fuck alone?" I reminded him of what a great a firefighter he was and that all the good work he was doing was not going unnoticed. "Bullshit, O'Brien! When they come I'm going to sic them onto the engine company. You can tell them how good you are at squirting water."

The Rescue was out on another call when the group of medical students arrived. The officer on the ladder company and I did our best to entertain them. Every single piece of equipment carried on both the engine and the ladder was shown. However, it was completely obvious that they were not interested in engine or ladder company operations.

I was on the apparatus floor when the Rescue returned. They were informed that the guests were waiting up in the kitchen. Walter went up to the third floor grumbling. I guess that the devil possessed him. He went to the kitchen by way of the pantry where he smeared peanut butter on the sole of his shoe, then proceeded to the kitchen. After placing his peanut buttered foot up on the table, he started to explain the various intricacies of the job. One young lady's eyes rolled up sideways in the direction of the lieutenant to come finally at rest on the peanut buttered sole. Her nose immediately started to twitch. Another future physician, after stammering a bit, said in a gentle voice, "Lieutenant, you may have stepped in something." Walter, hardly missing a beat, acknowledged their concern and then swiped his finger across the offending material and lodged it ceremoniously in his mouth. As he continued to explain the finer workings of the Rescue Squad, one by one the guests slowly departed. They never returned for a subsequent visit to headquarters.

Later the chief of the department heard from one of the hospital honchos that firefighters seemed a very peculiar lot. Especially the Rescue Squad.

Bones

Walter had a sense of humor that defied description. He spent much of his time on duty thinking up tricks to play on the guys in headquarters. Even though he was the lieutenant on the Rescue Company he still found time to play. As I said, headquarters was a beehive of activity because Engine 1, Rescue 1, Ladder 1, the division chief ran out of there and Fire Alarm was located in another wing of the building. Something was always doing, twenty-four hours a day.

    Walter spent some time up in Fire Alarm working on running cards. I was lieutenant of Engine 1 and rearing to go. This particular night I was sitting at the patrol desk making out the watch list. The phone rang and it was Fire Alarm informing me that a box was coming in. This means a full dispatch and companies would be rolling. Picking up the speaker phone I announced in a strong, clear voice, "Box coming in." The deputy chief was in quarters and I figured this would give him a head start. I no sooner had put the mike down when the door to the patrol room opened and in flew a large empty cardboard box. You didn't have to be a brain surgeon to know who was behind that corrugated tumbleweed! Walter followed the box in and was laughing his head off. He thought that was a great joke.

    One day the Rescue Company was returning from a run and Walter spotted his friend Henry who drove a rendering truck. Henry's job was to go around to stores and pick up bones and meat that the butchers couldn't use. He would have as many as make soap. On a summer day you could smell Henry's truck coming a mile away. The Rescue pulled up next to the meat wagon. Walter now persuaded Henry to give him a barrel of meat and bones. Now the pot thickened! Walter and the Rescue guys arranged the meat and bones on the stretcher and covered the mess up with a blanket. Walter now called Fire Alarm and told them that they were on the way to the City Hospital to pick up equipment. Of course, he also knew that there was a new intern on duty that day.

When they arrived at the hospital one of the guys went ahead and told the emergency room crew that they had a victim of an automobile accident on the way in. The litter was on the table. As the nurse pulled back the blanket, the Rescue guys were headed out the door. Walter just had to remain long enough to peek through the door to see the reaction. It was a strange combination of amazement, disgust, revulsion and laughter. The intern stared down at the sight before him and his jaw went slack. It was now time for Walter to go. As he ran down the hallway, a nurse was chasing him yelling, "I'll get you for this for this one, Walter!"

As the intern stared at the collage of bones and meat before him he was heard to utter, "Do you think we have all the parts yet?"

Fire Down Under

Harvard University has a maze of tunnels that connect many of the buildings. These tunnels are used to transport food and supplies from the main commissary building to various dining halls. During my high school years I worked at Harvard pushing food carts through this maze. Little did I ever know that one day I would be down there fighting a fire.

Normally nothing is stored in the tunnels because of the serious fire hazard. At the time of this fire I was lieutenant of Engine 1 and stationed at headquarters near Harvard Square. Underground fires are unique in many ways, and this particular fire stands out in my mind due to the difficulties we had in attempting to extinguish it.

The Rescue Company had been out of service most of the morning. All the heavy duty equipment had been removed and was on the rear apparatus floor. The mechanic said the truck had a broken spring and should be back in service by noon. Deputy Murphy told Walter to split his crew between Engine 1 and Ladder 1. Three men were assigned to the truck and Walter, the Rescue lieutenant, came with me. Walter and I had been friends for some time. He loved a good laugh and was a real prankster.

The box came in at 11:30. It was struck for smoke in the kitchen area of Leverett House, one of undergraduate residence halls on Boylston Street. We were the first company to arrive and were told by the Harvard Police that there was a slight smoke condition in the commissary kitchen. We laid a big line to the loading dock entrance. Now there was a great deal more than a slight smoke condition. I could hardly see the ceiling lights in the kitchen. The first alarm assignment had arrived, three engines and two trucks. After some investigation we determined that the seat of the heavy smoke was the complex of tunnels that connected the various halls, which in some cases were three quarters of a mile apart. Now the problem was to locate the fire!

The smoke was getting really thick now and had a distinct electrical odor. The commissary manager informed the chief that there were no food carts missing and everyone had been accounted for. He also offered the information that for the past week he had been getting complaints of an electrical odor in the tunnel system. The deputy called Fire Alarm and requested them to have a crew from the Cambridge Electric respond to the scene. There was no way to know how far the fire was in and how much hose we would need. There was also no way to effect ventilation. Ladder 1 set up a smoke ejector near the ramp leading to the tunnel. The division chief, who is incident commander, transmitted a 10-45, the working fire signal. The second responding chief was ordered to check the smoke conditions in the tunnel entrances. He reported that the furthermost entrance had a light haze and the conditions became worse as he moved toward the area of the fire.

We reduced our two and a half inch line using a two and a half by one and a half wye. Walter and his crew began to advance the line into the tunnel. We would back him up. At the time we were using 2.5 demand type Scott air masks. The air supplies in this type of self contained breathing apparatus was good for about thirty minutes, depending how hard you were working and using air. Walter advanced the line and we kept a hand on the hose. We had only gone a short distance when command called us with orders to return. When we re-entered the kitchen, conditions had become much worse. The heavy acrid smoke generated by whatever was burning had driven the command post out of the building. Chief Murphy told us that the power company had killed all circuits that ran through the maze. A representative of the college had also come to the scene with an updated map of the passageways. The turn toward the river was about seventy yards in and to the left. The tunnel ended at that point, but there were access ducts that carried telephone and electrical cable under the Charles River. We explained that visibility was zero down in that area.

By this time, the incident commander had requested and transmitted a second alarm. More smoke ejectors were set up to assist in ventilation so that we could get to the seat of the fire. Cambridge Electric told us that there had been electrical work going on near where two tunnels converge at Winthrop Hall. This time we entered carrying life lines and pushing a small cart with six CO_2 extinguishers. Ten steps inside I noted that the tunnel was hotter and visibility was still zero. If you held your gloved hand up to the face piece of the mask, you could not see it. Slowly we made our way into the uncertain darkness. Now the passageway was slopping downward. I remember wishing that I had paid more attention to the layout when I pushed carts through the dammed things during my high school days. We had changed cylinders and were good for about thirty minutes. Walter had the life line tied to him. He yelled, "Connie, I'm going to crawl a little farther to see if I can find any fire!" I told him that I was right behind him. All that I could see in front of my face piece was jet blackness. The heat was definitely building, which would indicate that we were approaching the fire. I took off my glove and held my bare hand as high as I could. It was hot air up there. The command post was keeping an eye on the time and our air supply. The problem was we would have to get back before running out of air.

The wall was turning left. I called to Walter but he did not reply. When I reached the pipe on the end of the hose I could see the smoke in front of my mask turning dull orange. Walter was nowhere in sight. I was groping for his life line with no success. He could be down or he could have fallen into a hole. The regulator on my tank was clicking like mad indicating that I was using entirely too much air. The panic was definitely building within me. I knew it but was having a hard time controlling it. Suddenly Walter stood beside me. He said it looked like wires along the side of the wall were burning. Then a commotion erupted behind me. One of the members on the line had started to hyperventilate. This can be very dangerous because the firefighter is probably depleting his air supply. Walter was now hitting the fire with the inch and a half line. Other guys moved up and were using the CO_2's. I could feel the hot steam. The hyperventilating guy was now in a state of panic. One of the Rescue crew told me it was Billy Stone, one of the new men. In the jet black darkness we struggled to calm him down, knowing there was a real danger that Billy could rip off his mask and suffocate quickly. It was imperative that we get him out of there and fast. As another man moved up on the line with Walter and began giving the fire a good hit, command informed us that we had about ten minutes of air remaining.

Which way is out? In the confusion I had become completely turned around. We told Billy that we were going out, and we began following the life line and, feeling the floor rise, we finally reached the ramp leading to the kitchen. His body was shivering uncontrollably. Conditions had improved considerably and the smoke had cleared. Billy was taken outside and given oxygen. Walter and the remainder of the crew had also come out. He reported to command that the fire had been knocked down and what he encountered down there. Another crew prepared to enter the tunnels to complete extinguishment and overhaul. When I went to check on Billy, he was OK but a little embarrassed. I told him not to worry about it and that I had had a close call too. We all have our moments of fear.

The fresh crew completed the extinguishment. About twenty five feet of heavy rubber insulation and pipe covering both sides of the tunnel had been burning and giving off unbelievable amounts of smoke. We remained at the scene for another two hours before we made up and returned to quarters. The smell of burnt rubber stayed around the station for quite awhile.

This tunnel fire is not typical of the jobs that we encounter on a daily basis. It was a reminder that during a tour of duty you never know what type of situation you will confront or the risks you may be asked to face.

WINE AND CHEESE

The call was for the odor of smoke in the fifth floor hallway of a building on Langdon Street about eight blocks from where I was stationed as lieutenant of Engine 4. Ladder 4 would be responding with us. It was a cool dry night, about 7:30 p.m. Upon arrival we found that there was nothing showing. Fire Alarm advised us that they had received another call stating that it smelled like burnt food. There *was* an odor of smoke. Ladder 4 was now with us and would check from the fifth floor to the roof. The odor was definitely stronger in the east wing.

Soon the smell was pinpointed to a specific apartment. When I knocked on the door we could hear people moving quickly inside the apartment. Finally a man opened the door but only as far as the security chain would allow. We did have the right place. There was a haze of smoke in there. I now asked the gentleman to allow us to enter. He wanted to know what our business was. He further stated that I would need a search warrant. I explained to him that the man standing beside me holding the ax had the search warrant in his hand. Now the gentleman opened the door.

Four people were in the room, two ladies and two gentlemen. I also noted that there was a roaring fire in the fireplace. It was also noted that until very recently the fireplace had been covered. Leaning against the couch was a four by four fireplace cover with a lovely floral design painted on it. There were also about twenty wood screws on the floor beside a screwdriver. Seat cushions were arranged neatly in a semicircle on the floor in front of the glowing fire. How nice! In the center of the circle was an arrangement of wine glasses and cheese. How delicious!

Now the officer of Ladder 4 was calling me on the radio saying that he had fire in the walls of the eighth floor. The pump operator of my company was also calling me to say that heavy fire was showing from the roof. How lovely!

"Engine Four calling Fire Alarm."

"Answering, Engine Four."

"On the orders of Lieutenant O'Brien, strike the box for forty three Langdon Street."

We ended up with a three alarm fire at 43 Langdon Street. When the chief asked the guy why he used the fireplace, he stated that it was there and he used it. When further asked if he ever considered why it was secured with twenty or so wood screws, he replied that it was fortunate he'd been able to find a screwdriver.

The chief looked at me and slowly shook his head. It was all in a day's work.

A Funeral Fire

The box came in about 2:00 p.m. Calls were being received for a fire in the Murphy Funeral Home in North Cambridge. The first company in, Engine 8, reported smoke and fire showing. Engine 8 and Ladder 4 are quartered about two blocks away and were quick to respond. Dave was on floor patrol downstairs and yelled up to us, "They've got smoke showing at box seven eight five two." This time of day usually was a good time to study for the captain's exam and I was tucked in a back room. The house work was done and we had a few hours to ourselves. Our company, Engine 1, responded on the second alarm. Then we heard, "C Three to Fire Alarm. On the orders of Deputy Chief Nazio strike the second alarm."

The funeral home was just across the street from the church that I attended. We responded up Concord Avenue from Harvard Square. The traffic was amazingly heavy for this time of day. After dropping a big line from Engine 9 we reported to the deputy in front of the building. Now I could see why the traffic was all tied up. A funeral was about to start. Cars were double-parked all over the place. The police were having their hands full. The hydrant on the corner of Huron and Concord was blocked by a funeral car. Heavy black smoke was now showing from the rear of the home. It had all the appearances of a first rate cellar fire. I also noted black smoke pushing from the gutter line and rising fast. This is a good indication that the fire is running the walls and is headed for the roof. Members of Engine 8 were advancing a line into the first floor by way of the front door. Engine 9 was ordered to stand by at the rear. The chief ordered us to force open the bulkhead door in the rear of the building and advance a big line into the cellar. A couple of ladder men made short work of the locked bulkhead door.

Just about then I heard a lot of yelling on the street. The chief was being told that two bodies were still inside the parlor. The woman who was scheduled to be buried today was still in the first floor rear. The body downstairs was still on the embalming table. Engine 8 was given the task of removing to safety the coffin that was supposed to be buried that morning. Lieutenant Duggan, assigned to Ladder 3, was off that day and happened to be in the neighborhood. By coincidence he also was related to the owner of the funeral home and was familar with the building. This building was a large two and a half story frame dwelling with aluminum siding. This type of siding tends to hold heat and fire in the building. Lieutenant Duggan offered to enter the building with Engine 8 and show them the easiest way to remove the deceased.

The fire had started as the result of a furnace problem and was going like hell in the rear section of the cellar. When they reached the coffin on the first floor, the smoke was so thick that the visibility was zero. Fire was breaking out of the baseboards. Flames were now showing on the rear walls. Fortunately, all hands were equipped with 2.5 Scott air masks. With some difficulty Lieutenant Duggan lowered the body into the coffin and closed the lid. After stumbling over floral arrangements they carried the coffin out of the building. I suppose it looked a bit strange to see firefighters carrying a coffin up the street.

While all this was going on we had our hands full in the cellar. The minute that the ladder guys popped the metal bulkhead door we were hit by a blast of heat. We backed down the stairs to block the heat from our faces. When we reached the cellar floor all that I could see was fire in front of my face piece. The line was charged and we hit the ceiling to cool things down. Speedy and I started working the line down what felt like a hallway leading toward the front of the building. The ladder guys were trying, but this fire was not venting. I could hear glass breaking somewhere. The heat was becoming unbearable. Engine 4 was behind us on a back-up line. They were hitting the ceiling just above us and we were able to hold our position. The cold water spraying down on us helped. Ladder 1 was given the task of finding the other body. The Rescue Company had already located the embalming room and gently covered the table. It was a case of defending in place. We did not allow the fire to endanger the deceased. The heavy volume of fire was knocked down in the boiler room and in an adjoining storage area. The first alarm companies overhauled the basement area. The fire did spread into the walls and ceiling of the basement. We were assigned to work with Ladder 4. We used salvage covers, which were large canvas tarps, to help limit the damage during overhaul operations.

Lieutenant Duggan was highly commended in general orders for his assistance at this fire while off duty. We were ordered to make up and return to quarters. I think that we all had a good feeling after this fire. This was a delicate, unusual situation that the members handled with respect and compassion.

Our Neighbor

During the 60s I was stationed as a lieutenant at Engine 6 on River Street. It was primarily a tenement area with narrow streets. During the winter months getting around the congested district could be a nightmare. This was a busy station and I caught quite a bit of action while stationed there—the riots in Harvard Square and the Prison Point Bridge fire to name just two. River Street ran from the Charles River to Central Square. Most of our neighbors were black. Living next to the station was an elderly black lady named Sara. I never saw her without a smile on her face. On hot and sticky days she would sit on the rear porch and read her Bible. Occasionally we could hear her singing an ancient spiritual. Our rear kitchen was about twenty feet from her yard. The bells never seemed to bother her. Every Sunday we would see her, splendidly dressed in her finest clothes, on the way to church.

One afternoon we heard an awful commotion in Sara's house. Then we heard her call, "Oh boys! Come quick and help me!" When we entered the parlor we found Sara on top of a not too steady piano bench with a broom in her hand. She was waving frantically at the floor. There it was, a big rat running around the room. It was probably trying to get away from the broom that was flying around. Sara was a big woman, and at the moment I was more concerned about the piano stool than the rodent. We finally showed the rat the door and turned our attention to Sara. She was scared stiff, but after a while we were able to calm her down.

Occasionally she would spend a morning making donuts, and she always gave us a dozen or so. One morning when I reported for work the apparatus was there but the men were missing. It had snowed heavily during the night. Sara had come into the station at about seven and said she was sitting in her kitchen and the floor started to sag. The lieutenant called Fire Alarm and put the company out of service; he also asked for a ladder truck. The kitchen was a one story extension with a flat roof. Apparently the weight of the snow had caused the kitchen to pull away from the house. Ladder 3 was able to brace the extension and stop the sag. Sara retreated to the front parlor and was giving us verbal encouragement. The rest of us took to the roof and started shoveling. Soon we had all the snow removed. Ladder 3 provided a salvage cover and made a temporary repair to the opening where the extension joined the roof. We checked for leaks in the gas and water pipes. Sara was as happy as a bluebird in spring. She kept repeating, "God bless you boys! Oh my, God bless you boys!" over and over.

A couple of the guys who were handy with tools decided that the kitchen required a more permanent repair. The project was completed on the first warm day. Everyone had some wood left over from completed home repair projects, and a couple of the guys purchased nails and angle braces. Sara gave a big hug and a kiss to all.

Every Sunday we could expect some sort of goodies with our coffee. However, one Sunday there were no goodies on the table. One of the boys went into the back yard and called, "Hey, Sara, are you okay?" There was no answer. They forced the kitchen door open and found Sara. She would not be going to church this morning; she had gone on to heaven.

Members of Engine Company 6 in full dress uniform

attended Sara's wake at the Spears Funeral Home on Western Avenue. Her head was slightly tilted toward the mourners and there was a smile on her face. It was as if she was saying, "These are my boys. Yes, these are my boys."

An Unfunny Valentine

My new assignment as lieutenant of Engine 6 involved many changes for me. This was not my neighborhood. West Cambridge was a maze of narrow one way streets that connected into other one way streets. When we pulled out of quarters we were on River Street headed east toward Central Square. If the box or still alarm was for the West Side, we had to go against the traffic flow for at least a block.

The division chief had just picked up the morning reports when the box came in. It was being struck for a building fire on Valentine Street. We were second due engine company. As we worked our way down the narrow streets I could see the brown dirty smoke plume rising into the sky. Ladder 3 was reporting off with smoke showing from a complex of one and two story, wood frame manufacturing buildings.

Valentine Plastics was a wholesale distributor of all sorts of plastic such as Lucite, Polyvinalchloride, and large piles were stored in the cellars of various buildings. This plastic came in 4'x 8' sheets, rolls of clear material used for covering and wrapping; various size rolls and tubes used in the medical profession. All of this material was stored in basements and in sheds. The showroom displayed finished products such as handles made of Bakerlite and plastic tubes used for various purposes. The front of the main showroom was located on Valentine Street. The deputy chief was on Brookline Street waiting for us. He ordered a big line into the rear yard and reduced it to an inch and a half. Engine 2 was already in the yard and was advancing their line into the cellar. At this point the fire involved only one building. However, this would change.

All that we carried for respiratory protection when this fire occurred were two MSA all service masks on the hose wagon and one CHEMOX type mask on the pump. The MSAs were rated for 16% oxygen and 3% poison gases and were not the best respiratory protection in a basement.

The fire was spreading uncontrolled in the cellar. Thick, black, tar-like smoke was making visibility zero. Engine 2 attempted to advance their line, but they were stopped. As we dragged our line down the narrow aisle between pallets of plastic pipe, there was a muffled explosion up ahead of us. It was not humanly possible to hold our position. Even with my face on the cold cement floor I could not breathe. That invisible hand was at my throat again, choking me. Engine 2 was backing out and dragging the line with them.

The fire was now a third alarm and had communicated to adjoining buildings. We were ordered to reposition and cover exposures. As we passed the loading dock, rolling clouds of dark orange and black flame were being pushed thirty feet into the yard. Multiple alarm companies were setting up for large stream appliances. The lieutenant of Engine 2 reported that he was missing a man. It was the pipeman, Steve Kelley.

Engine 9 was running lines into their wagon deck gun and we gave them a hand. Now the question was could we hold our position in the yard? Three storage buildings were now involved and the fire was totally out of control. The rescue companies were able to get into where Kelley was last seen. He was found face down in a pool of water. I saw him when they lugged him out. His face was jet black. I don't think that he was breathing.

The flame coming from the loading dock was now like a

blow torch. Heavy lines were directed to wet down the adjacent three story frame dwellings. These clapboard and tar shingled structures were now smoking. All interior firefighting was abandoned. It was becoming increasingly difficult to hold our position even outside on the wagon deck gun. The black smoke would cut your heart out.

After all exposures were protected, fresh engine companies again moved into the involved buildings. We were told to take a break and we found the Salvation Army canteen truck on Brookline Street. The hot soup tasted great! Chief Mulberry then told us to reposition our big line to the front of the main showroom on Valentine Street. The main body of fire had been knocked down, and we now moved into a surround and drown operation. Insidious white fumes were still rising from the partly burnt and melted plastics in the cellars.

We had been at the fire for about four hours when two men who had been allowed through the police line approached me. One asked how long we had been fighting this fire, and I told him about four hours. "Do you have any idea what the products of combustion were?" he asked. Now I asked him who they were and why were they interested. They identified themselves as chemical engineers from MIT and had been informed of the fire. According to them we had already inhaled sufficient toxic fumes to be in real danger. Hmm! I directed the two academics to the command post to explain the developments to the chief of the department. Forty-eight firefighters were sent to various hospitals to be examined for possible smoke-chemical poisoning. None of my crew went, which was probably a mistake on our part. Now, years later, I wish that we had gone. Back then eating smoke was an accepted part of the job and that was that!

Fire fighter Kelley eventually came around and spent three weeks in the hospital. He never returned to duty. He had sustained permanent damage to his lungs.

We were relieved at the fire and returned to the firehouse to wash up and then go home. As usual the kids met me at the door full of stories of the day. Upstairs in the kitchen Peggy asked, "Did you have anything today?"

I replied, "Just a smudge, hon. Just a smudge."

The Prison Point Bridge

Where Boston and Cambridge come together in the East Cambridge section of the city there is a very large freight yard. The Prison Point Bridge spanned the yards between the Charlestown neighborhood of Boston and Cambridge for a distance of approximately one mile. On the Boston side the area was formerly known as Cherry Point. Years ago a large prison had been located there. They'd had an electric chair and were not afraid to use it. The only remnants of the prison is the name Prison Point Bridge.

In 1969 a reclamation plant was operating on the Cambridge side of the bridge. Vast amounts of rubbish were collected and brought to the plant where hydraulic machinery compressed the trash into five foot by three foot bales. The idea of reclamation was in its infancy. The month of August had been hot and sticky. We hadn't had any appreciable rain for quite some time. For weeks a labor dispute in the disposal industry had been dragging on. Normally the bales would be taken by freight train and loaded aboard barges daily. However, due to a strike the bales of rubbish were allowed to be stored in the vicinity of the plant and under the bridge. There were thousands of them. It was not long before the residents of both Charlestown and lower East Cambridge were complaining about the stench. The reclamation plant continued to handle the large volume of refuge trucked into the plant. Both the newly compressed bales and the already stored bales were liberally sprayed with a liquid concoction that eliminated the smell for the most part and took care of the mosquito population. Unfortunately, since the liquid was also highly combustible, this also created a time bomb with a fuse.

The spark that lit the fuse was provided at about 4:00 p.m. on a weekday. Box 1265 was transmitted for the report of a rubbish fire in the yard of the reclamation plant. It could have been a carelessly discarded cigarette or rats and matches. Who knows? Engine 3 was located about four blocks from the freight yard on Gore Street. They were the first to arrive and found a small fire involving some rubbish quite near the sea of baled paper. Before they could run a booster to contain and extinguish the fire, the wind whipped the flames directly up and over the bales. When the commanding officer of Engine 5 arrived at the scene he immediately saw the danger. Without hesitation he ordered a working fire, which was followed shortly by a request for a second alarm. Now the sky was jet black. Giant plumes of acrid smoke rose hundreds of feet. The sun was completely hidden. The wind whipped flames now were racing across the bales. There was no way of stopping the massive spread of fire. The flammable fluid that had been sprayed on the tops of the bales was now acting as the catalyst for the impending disaster that would follow.

A strong southwest wind was driving the flames across the freight yard toward Boston. Now the underside of the bridge was burning. The dry creosote wooden framing was burning furiously. A stiff dry wind now was blowing the fire across the tops of the bales toward the freight sheds in Charlestown. All the makings of a very serious fire were in place.

I had left the house a little early for work. Lieutenant Morse had something doing and asked me to come in a little early. I was at the traffic light at the corner of Memorial Drive and

River Street waiting to make a left turn. The cop directing at the intersection spotted my uniform and pointed his finger at me to go. He also was excited and pointing to my left. After making the turn onto River Street I immediately saw what he was trying to tell me. The sky was jet black. It was like a gigantic cloud edged in dark blue. Engine 6 had already responded on the second alarm. Just as I entered the station the third alarm was striking on the tapper. The radio traffic was brisk. The chief in charge was directing apparatus to approach the fire from various directions. He was desperately trying to get ahead of the fire. I could easily detect the urgency in his voice. The other members of the night shift had arrived and we piled into my car for the trip to the fire. When we got there most of the bales of paper were now involved. The fire had also extended to large metal clad storage buildings where the paper was baled. The buildings were also filled with burning debris. The fire had also begun to feed on the wooden creosote underpinning of the bridges. We found our hose wagon parked on the Cambridge side of the bridge. All the hose, twenty four lengths, had been taken off. When I put my boots on I made the mistake of leaving my shoes on the bridge next to the wagon. When the fire took hold of the bridge the wagon was moved to a point of safety. Alas, my shoes were not moved and I never saw them again. They were destroyed! We were informed that our company was operating a two and a half inch line along the railroad tracks on the lee side of the bridge. Visibility on that side was zero due to the smoke. We followed the line down the tracks but could not see a foot in front of us. The heat was now almost unbearable. The entire length of the bridge was burning. Boston had struck a multiple alarm on the fire. Now we were crawling between the rails of the track following the hose line toward the bridge, and then I could feel boots in front of me. Lieutenant Morse and Bobby Foley were working the line and the third man was backing them up. We were not wearing masks. Even with my head pressed into the dirt it was impossible to escape from the thick black acrid smoke. Lieutenant Morse was yelling to me to give them a hand backing the line away from the fire. They could no longer hold this position. Gigantic sheets of flame were now rolling over our heads. Very shortly we would be pinned down by the flame and unable to escape. Now we were being hit by a stream of water from the rear. Another company had moved up the tracks to cover our retreat. Leaving the line where it was and with our heads down we crawled back, single file under the protection of water stream. The controlling nozzle was closed and we started to pull the line back down the track. Even with adequate help, moving a charged hose line can be a formidable task. Suddenly, a searing blast of heat pinned us flat between the tracks. My nose was now against the railroad ties and broken glass. The Federal Liquor Company warehouse was about twenty five feet to our left. Naturally, the place was full of alcohol and if it went we'd all go with it. Behind us we could hear the rumble of smaller explosions. All hell was breaking loose! Even though we were outside, I could not see my hand in front of my face.

It was now becoming very difficult to breathe. The smoke would cut your heart out. A ladder pipe was being set up near the tracks. Someone got hold of a hose clamp and clamped our line shut, then a chief ordered us to connect the line into the ladder pipe Siamese. Even though it was still daylight and even with high beams on, visibility was zero. It was necessary to have a man walk in front of the arriving engines to guide them through the smoke. Another two big lines were run into the Siamese. Now the ladder pipe is sweeping a section of the bridge. The range of application was limited and they were doing little good. The fire was now seriously exposing the potato sheds on the Charlestown side of the railroad tracks, and they began rearranging lines to cover the new threat.

Fighting this type of fire can present problems. The fire has not been contained and is spreading. Established positions of defense must be abandoned. You must save the lines that you can, then drag them, full of water, to the new defensive position. In many cases this takes time. Unfortunately, the fire will not wait. It will move on. It will move in the direction of the wind—and in this case the fire was creating its own wind—and will feed on all combustibles in its path. This particular fire was moving very fast, and if it wasn't controlled in time, it would certainly gain conflagration proportions.

Additional engine companies were setting up on the Boston side. A desperate fight between man and the element of fire was now in progress. We had our hands full where we were. Water was fast becoming a major problem. Other engine companies were setting up to relay water from other water mains. Lines had been already connected into the sprinkler system of the Federal Liquor warehouse. Flames were now impinging on the sides of the walls facing the burning bridge. Fortunately, the building had been designed and constructed for its use and there were no windows facing the fire.

The bridge was very old and was constructed with large creosote soaked timbers, which accounted for much of our problems with smoke. We worked the fire all night long, spending most of the night on top of freight cars, operating a two and a half inch line. At about 7:30 next morning the fire was declared under control. The Boston boys had succeeded in covering the exposures on the lee side and were holding. Heavy stream appliances had covered the wooden potato sheds with water. They were destined to burn about a year later.

The bridge itself was a total loss. Thousands of bales of paper had been consumed. Five buildings were burnt to the ground. Many surrounding cities had sent mutual aid assistance. Just after the day crew was dismissed, someone told me that there was trouble back at my pump. A large trailer truck had crossed the fire lines without permission and taken down some power lines and these lines were now draped across our pumper. When I arrived at the pump the operator, Billy Ridgley, was quite upset with the truck driver. As I was playing my peace maker role, someone said, "Connie, what the hell's wrong with your eyes? They're almost swollen shut." Then suddenly I could not see a dammed thing.

The ride to the Massachusetts General Hospital was uneventful. In the emergency room I laid on the table under the glaring bright lights—which I could hardly see. Someone was prying my eye open, but I couldn't make him out. My eyes felt like big cotton balls. My boots and rubber coat had been removed. Someone was pouring a liquid into my eyes. It is very strange the way you can hear better when your eyes aren't working too well. The medical personnel were discussing another case of closed eyes. In fact, they were discussing another member of my engine company who was on a table in another room. They poured a cooling solution into my eyes for about thirty minutes, which was followed by bandaging. When they finished with me I looked like a masked rider. Both the eyes had gauze on them held in place by some kind of tape. The doctor told me that the smoke from the burning creosote had irritated the eyes to such an extent that they refused to take any more and closed tight. He then told me I'd be able to see fine in about a week. Hmmmmm. The fellow on the other table turned out to be Joe Scanlon and his diagnosis was the same as mine. I remembering hearing the doctor talking to someone else and commenting that they should also check our lungs for possible damage. When I look back at those days I think the doctors must have considered us crazy to do work like that. Maybe they were right!

They led us to a car and back to Engine 6. Boston Engine 34 from Brighton was covering us. I had a cup of fresh coffee and a doughnut. One of the Boston guys had gone out to the bakery. Paul Flynn drove me home. Once again I stood at the foot of the stairs and asked if all the kids were in bed. Peg thanked Paul and took my arm. Again I will say that the true soldiers are not in the trenches but stand there, upright and as sweet as a rose, at the head of the stairs.

The Aku Aku

We had a large Asian restaurant known as the Aku Aku in the western section of Cambridge. It was located on Route 2, near where the city of Cambridge and the towns of Arlington and Belmont come together. During its heyday, the Aku Aku was an extremely popular restaurant and lounge. Handy next door was a motel.

When I was a new lieutenant and assigned to float between two engine companies, it was my duty to know as much as I could about the areas they covered. The Aku Aku was within the first alarm response area of Engine 4. Originally this building was a one story, 150 foot by 75 foot warehouse. It was of second class construction—wood and cement block. The long front of the structure faced Route 2, a main east to west highway.

When I inspected this area, the building was undergoing a major renovation with a second story being added. In fact, the structure was being transformed into the Aku Aku. As we proceeded with the inspection, we noted that the second story was a maze of wooden structural components. I do remember noting that if this place ever burned and the fire got a good hold of the wood frame construction, it would really go. About four years later, when I was still a lieutenant and assigned to Engine 6, the Aku Aku did go.

It was during the summer months and vacations were in full

swing. When I reported to Engine 6 to start a night tour, the officer whom I was relieving told me that would I lose my pump operator because he was being detailed to act as aid to the chief of department. We usually had five men for duty, so now I had four. No big deal, I thought. Billy Ridgley would fill in as pump operator and Charlie Brodrick would drive the hose wagon. Things were quite until 7:00 p.m. I was up in the office trying to determine why the fuel we received during the month didn't add up. We were usually close, but for some reason this month the figures were a mile off. This kind of imbalance usually happened because of fuel we received at a fire scene. The only trouble with that theory was that the month had been quiet and without multiple alarms. We hadn't received any fuel at any scenes. I could hear some activity on the radio downstairs at the patrol desk, but I couldn't make it out. Then I heard box 7841 begin striking for a building fire on Route 2. Engine 6 is located in the Cambridgeport section of the city and quite a distance from Route 2. Billy called up the sliding pole hole that we didn't go until the third alarm. I slid the pole to the apparatus floor and just as I was arriving at the patrol desk Engine 4 was giving a radio report: "Engine Four calling Fire Alarm. We have heavy smoke showing from the roof of Aku Aku." Fire Alarm acknowledged them. Almost immediately Engine 4 reported a working fire. Then we heard, "C Two calling Fire Alarm."

"Answering, C Two."

"On the orders of Deputy Chief Rogan, strike a second alarm on box seven eight four one." C2 then reported that heavy fire was blowing through the roof of an occupied restaurant. This meant that much of the first alarm assignment would be committed to search and rescue. The firefighting operations will not be abandoned, of course. As experienced firefighters we know very well that properly placed hose lines will ultimately save lives.

I was on my way to the kitchen for a quick cup of coffee when the third alarm was requested. We put on our gear, climbed onto the apparatus, and off we roared. We had various routes we could take to North Cambridge from Cambridgeport; the choice of the route depended on the time of day. It was early evening, so we used Memorial Drive. The radio was alive with messages as we made our way to Route 2—"charge this line...more pressure on that line...." We had an open cab and I was trying to hear if we were being ordered to come into the scene via a particular route. This was difficult due to the roar of the diesel engine. However, a chief was waiting on Route 2 for us when we arrived. He ordered me to find a hydrant and drop a two and a half to the front door.

Now we had a problem. All the available hydrants were taken by the second alarm companies. We were forced to locate the pump a good distance away from the fire. We now laid the big line to a Belmont Fire Department engine that needed more water. The place was really cooking. Heavy acrid black smoke was pouring out of every nook and crevice. A ladder company was smashing out the plate glass windows in the front. We took a line off Engine 4 located in front and advanced into the bar area. Even with the windows out the smoke still hung about two feet from the floor. After pushing ahead through overturned bar stools, I could make out the door leading from the bar to the main hallway. We were wearing Scott 2.2 air SCBAs with thirty minute air cylinders. The sound coming from the door ahead of us was like a fast moving freight train. It was the roar of the fire in the main restaurant area. Ladder men were with us and they started to pull the ceiling. Now the visibility was zero. We had fire up there and started to hit it. Every time the hook went through the ceiling you could see heavy fire.

Another company was working the line in the hallway in front of us. Suddenly, I heard a low rumbling noise that was followed by a blast of superheat and flame that came from the hallway and blew over our heads. The first working companies had advanced a big line down the hallway and were attacking the fire in the main restaurant. A large air conditioning duct, about six beet by four feet, had been installed up in the ceiling of the hallway. The fire had damaged the wooden structural supports, causing the duct to collapse, crashing through the ceiling and landing directly in the corridor. Now they had heavy fire in front of them and the only escape route was blocked.

The company in front of us was backing out. Conditions had deteriorated. The feeling that it was getting ready to blow began to flow through me. Someone was yelling at me through his mask that two companies were trapped down the hallway. There was another rumble but not as strong as the first, then I head someone near the entrance, about thirty feet behind us, yelling, "Back out! Back out!" I was near the door leading to the hallway and could feel the tin duct that had collapsed. It was blocking the hallway. We heard someone yelling, "Mayday! Mayday!" We realized that someone was inside the duct and the laddermen started to bang on the sides of the duct with their axes. We knew we had brothers inside and we would not leave without them. Word about what had happened was relayed back outside and more help started to come to us. The bells on all our air cylinders were ringing and we had to leave or we'd run out of air.

Six frightened and happy to be alive firefighters were pulled out of that duct. Three of them were in very bad shape. They all had run out of air and put their mask hoses inside of their rubber coats to get the last of the available air. It was a very close call for them. Lieutenant Bill Kelly of Engine 4 and another man were the most seriously injured. They had almost suffocated. The other four firefighters were treated for smoke inhalation and released.

The fire at the Aku Aku became a surround and drown job. However, even though the building suffered extensive structural damage, it was renovated and operated as a night club for several years. Today the building stands vacant, a silent sentinel to a valiant firefight.

A View from the Window

It was the last thing you did before lying down. A quick look out the second floor rear window would tell you if there was work undone. Engine 2 and Ladder 3 are a busy house located on Mass. Ave. at Lafayette Square. When I took over command of Engine 2 my predecessor told me a few tricks. Looking out the rear window was one of them. Stolen cars would be abandoned on Erie Street and set on fire. This usually happened between midnight and three in the morning and could easily be seen from the second floor looking west.

Eventually someone would either pull a box or call the police. Getting a head start helped as the fire could spread to other abandoned cars. Motor vehicle fires can present some very serious problems: the rupture of fuel tanks from the heat could engulf a firefighter; exploding tires can cause serious injury; and gases given off by burning imitation leather seat covering can contain toxic components.

I looked out the window and there it was, a dull orange glow in the sky. As I headed for the pole the phone at the patrol desk was ringing. It was Fire Alarm dispatching the engine and ladder to an automobile fire on Pacific Street. It was going good and as we pulled up a tire let go with a bang. The car had been abandoned and all the windows were broken. The ladder guys gave us a hand running the attack inch and three quarter line. We were making good progress on the fire when Henry Santos told me that there was a dead body in the rear seat. I learned long ago that the guys like to kid around. They've been known to stuff a mannequin in a car as a joke. However, when Jack Kenney also told me a body was in the rear seat, I became a believer. Jack was not the kidding type.

The victim was sitting upright in the back seat. Then someone noticed that he had a bullet hole in his right temple. Ordinarily a division chief would not respond to a routine auto fire. This, however, was not an ordinary car fire. Due to our discovery in the backseat, I asked for the deputy chief and the police. It was a cold raw and rainy night. The police were busy and slow to respond. It was raining harder and I could think of a million places that I'd rather be. When the police finally arrived they determined that what we thought was a bullet hole was in fact a piece of burnt material.

The victim turned out to be a young man about twenty five. He had a drinking problem and had been refused a room at the shelter. The shelter consisted of two construction trailers located a couple of blocks away. I guess that the guy was bad news and the couple who ran the shelter wanted no part of him. Between his feet we found cans of sterno that he had been using to keep warm. There was a bottle of cheap whiskey on the floor. Apparently he had crawled inside the car to get out of the weather. He may have fallen asleep and spilled the whiskey on his lap. The lit cans of sterno did the rest.

We returned to quarters and, after making out the required reports, I sat in the office and looked out at the desolate rain swept square. With five sons of my own, many questions, concerns and possibilities were running through my mind. Where was the help this still young man needed? Could he have been saved? Unanswered questions that did not concern me directly, but...do. My silent reflection was interrupted by the alert signal striking box 3479 for a building fire. The job doesn't stop.

GREEN STREET

I had been the captain of Engine 2 for only about three months and much of the company paperwork remained a bit of a mystery. Consequently, making out the monthly reports could be a big pain in the rear end for me. Usually most of it could be done by the day officer and the officer working the night tour would draw up a rough draft and all the night officer had to do was to fill in his shift information. The day crew had been at a fire most of the day, however, and little had been accomplished on the monthlies.

The alarm came in at 6:30. Box 363 was transmitted for a building fire at the corner of Green and Pearl Streets. As I slid the pole my mind was making a mental picture of the area. The rear entrances of a mattress factory, large furniture stores, and a few barrooms are on Green Street. Now Fire Alarm was calling the division chief and saying that the police were on the scene and reporting a fire in the rear entry of the mattress factory. As we turned onto Green Street I could see the reflection of flames against the tenement houses across the street. Then I had a good look at it. The mattress factory was a four story second class building. A loading platform extended the full width of the building. The showroom was at the front on Mass. Ave. On the corner of Green and Pearl Streets there was a nightclub that occupied the first and second floors.

We were greeted by a gigantic ball of fire that completely

involved the loading dock area. The pump located at a hydrant at the corner of Green and Pearl Streets and we dropped two big lines and connected them into the wagon deluge gun. I called the pump and ordered the lines charged as quickly as possible. The previous night a snowstorm had dropped about eight inches on the city. Normally this would not interfere with our operations. Not this time, however. This was not to be a routine job.

Deputy Chief Tim O'Donnell had already ordered a second and third alarm. He yelled across the street to me, "Connie, let's get some water on it!" Just then the pump operator called me with the news that the hydrant had been hit and broken off at the base. Some thoughtful truck driver had stood it up nicely in the snow. Probably a city snow plow! Years ago a damaged hydrant would send water skyward for about twenty feet, but new hydrants have a disconnect coupling. I crossed the street and informed the chief. He shook his head, saying, "It's going to be one of those nights, Connie." We now had flame lapping into the second floor window. A company located in the front of the building was calling that they had heavy fire inside the furniture store.

The multiple alarm chief located at the front of the building on the Mass. Ave. Due to the extent of the fire, Chief O'Donnell had quickly ordered four alarms. Now the telephone poles were going and hot wires were dropping all over the place. Engine 6, responding up Pearl Street, heard the situation that we were in and laid two big feeder lines into us. This allowed us to get our gun working, but by now the wind generated by the heat was turning the 500 gallons per minute stream sideways.

Deep rumbles emanated from within the building and we knew that something had let go. A ball of fire and jet black smoke rolled end over end skyward. To make matters worse the wind was blowing toward the interior of the building and Mass. Ave. A sight such as this never fails to cause a firefighter to feel a clutching fear in his heart.

The chief of the department ordered me to take an engine company into the adjoining building and check for extension of fire, saying, "Captain, if you have fire in there, let me know and we'll get you some help." We forced entry and advanced our line. It was hot and smokey but we could see. Our 4.5 Scott masks would give us about twenty minutes of air depending on our breathing rate. We had a ladder company with us and they were dragging a flood light in with them. We could hear glass breaking somewhere and the lieutenant of the ladder company said that they were probably taking out the windows in the front. We had advanced about half the depth of the building and there still was no sign of fire, but the smoke was getting thicker and banking down. Using my portable I reported my findings to the chief. He ordered me to stand by and report any extension through the firewall. Visibility was fading. There was still no visible fire. The smoke lifted a bit and I could see the front of the building. I told my men that I was going toward the front. The smoke was much lighter now and there was good visibility. Bobby Kelley was with me as we walked cautiously down the center aisle toward the front. We had not gone far when the smoke level dropped to the floor. We couldn't see our hands in front of our masks. Looking to my right I could see and hear flame breaking through the wall. Using the portable I reported the extension. We retraced our steps back to rear of the showroom. My company was advancing the big line toward us. We dragged the line to a position where we could hit the fire coming through the wall. The chief had ordered two more engine companies to advance lines to cover us and hit the fire. The low air alarms began sounding in our SCBAs—self-contained breathing apparatus. When the low air alarm goes off you still have enough air to exit the building. This must be done without delay because when your air is gone it is gone—and you will suffocate.

Out in the street the hustle and bustle of a firefight were in full progress. Five alarms had been sounded and companies were busy going to work. The fire had gotten into the mattress storage area and the smoke being generated was thick and acrid. At the front of the building firefighters needed masks to hold their positions.

My three sons, two of whom are now Nashua, New Hampshire firefighters, were with me that night. Now my concern was, Where the hell are they? They were members of the auxiliary fire department which at the time had quarters in the north section of the city. Engines 11 and 12 were assigned to the auxiliary. They would cover on multiple alarms and on greater alarms would respond to the fire. A friend told me that the three of them were up on the roof so I climbed up to check on them. My three sons greeted me with "Hi, Dad!" as they operated a big line from a partially collapsed roof. Their faces were black from the tar smoke and I could only see the whites of their eyes. We all descended the ladder together. Michael was chanting, "Gee, Dad, we were okay!" Neal was the last one off and was saying, "One more lick, Dad, one more lick." I could never explain to their mother if they were hurt. Sternly, in my strongest paternal tone, I ordered them to remain outside. As I walked away I heard, "One more lick! Gee, dad!" Later, Timothy, the youngest, told me that my line of work was not for him. "Don't tell my brothers," he said, "but I wasn't exactly comfortable up there." I explained to him that not everyone was cut out to be a firefighter and it was OK. Today Tim is a Cambridge police officer and is assigned to the motorcycle squad.

The lads were getting the upper hand on the fire. More and

more black sooty smoke was being replaced with clouds of steam. My company was assigned overhaul duty. I was up on the second floor of the nightclub checking for hot spots when I spotted Deputy Chief Charlie Stewart standing in the doorway. He said that he had a sore throat from the acrid smoke and he wanted to know if there was a glass of cold water handy. "We've got some soothing syrup behind the bar, Deputy." He sat on a barstool while I searched for a suitable syrup to soothe his parched and smoke burnt throat. At last I found it, tucked behind a bottle of Old Kentucky Horse Urine and a fifth of Indian Moonlight. The ice in the chest was still good so we were all set to rest a bit and contemplate a job well done.

A decorative canopy covered the bar area in an effort to create the atmosphere of an outdoor market or cafe. It happened quickly and this was a blessing. We were just about ready to raise our glasses when the canopy, which was completely filled with water and debris, let go, spilling its entire contents on top of us. The canopy ran the full length of the bar and split right over our heads. Needless to say the soothing syrup was ruined. The force of the deluge almost knocked us off our seats. It was clearly time to depart. Chief Stewart said the syrup had been watered down.

Out on the street, companies were starting to make up. Someone told me the coffee truck was on Mass. Ave. I knew, though, that somehow coffee would just taste like coffee and...oh well.

From Russia Without Love

The call was for a suicide on Mass. Ave. The top-heavy Rescue unit rocked as it made its way toward the scene. Lieutenant Raft held onto the passenger seat. A million and one thoughts were causing pressure to build within his head.

Fire Alarm called and said to stand by on Channel 13. This is a fire priority channel used mostly by command officers on the fireground. A light rain was falling causing an eerie glare on the pavement. Fire Alarm said, "Rescue, this incident involves a Russian national who jumped out a second floor window. The Cambridge Police are at the scene and are reporting this is a sensitive situation."

As the Rescue pulled over to the curb, the lieutenant noted at least four Cambridge police cruisers and also members of the Harvard University police. The Rescue crew made their way through the crowd and found a middle-aged man who had apparently jumped or fallen from a window. He was lying on the cement walkway and was bleeding profusely from his mouth. Two men were yelling at the him in Russian and trying to get him to his feet.

Cambrdige and Harvard police, however, were attempting to allow the Rescue crew to examine the man. A Cambridge police captain told Lieutenant Raft that the man was a Russian agent and he had jumped out the window in an attempt to escape from the other two Russian men. The jumper was in obvious pain and with all the confusion it was difficult to conduct an evaluation. Raft could tell the man had a serious head injury and probably internal injuries. He was trying, struggling to say something. He grabbed the fire lieutenant by the collar, pulled his head down and said in broken English, "Get me out of here quick. They try to kill me." The lieutenant was stunned by the jumper's statement.

After some pushing and shoving of the agents, the Rescue was able to prepare the victim for transport and get the man on the litter. Now the Russians demanded that they be allowed to accompany the man to the hospital. This request was denied. Cambridge police officers, however, did accompany the man in the Rescue unit.

The press was waiting for them at the door to the emergency room. Representatives of the Russian government were also there. After being denied permission to talk to the jumper, they attempted to get details from the Rescue members. Some of the agents were very belligerent and demanding.

When the Rescue returned to quarters, the lieutenant called the deputy chief and informed him of the incident. The remainder of the tour was uneventful until about eleven o'clock when Lieutenant Raft got a phone call from a reporter who wanted to know the particulars of the incident. The lieutenant told him to get a copy of the incident report from headquarters in the morning. When the lieutenant arrived home the next morning, his wife said that a foreign sounding man had called and would call back. However, the man never called and the incident was closed.

From time to time Lieutenant Raft would try to determine the outcome of this incident, but he was never successful. Each time he asked he would get a reply like, "Raft, what you don't know will never hurt you!" An incident such as this points out the fact that you never know what is coming when you put your turnout gear on the apparatus. Perhaps it is just as well.

Sizzle in the Snow

Two days after the 1978 blizzard things were still far from normal. It had snowed for three days and the city was under emergency conditions. We were still holding extra men on duty in the city. There was a serious problem with blocked fire hydrants. In the City of Cambridge, in spite of the public works department doing their best, clearing the streets of snow is always a major problem. Cambridge has many narrow streets, some of which were laid out during colonial times, so even in good weather responding to alarms is a task. When a snowstorm is imminent, a parking ban is placed in effect in areas marked by signs that read "Snow Emergency" and the police tow illegally parked cars to allow the plows to operate. Cars are parked on both sides of narrow streets and a bulldozer is used to clear a lane. The passage of fire apparatus is virtually impossible. Often it's necessary to hand lay lines and carry ladders and equipment to the fire building, and, of course, the ladder trucks get hung up on corners due to insufficient room to maneuver.

At the time of the big storm my normal duty station was Lafayette Square where I was captain of Engine 2. When I reported for duty at 5:00 p.m. I was told that I was detailed to cover the Division Two Car. This is the downtown area closest to Boston. The regular chief had called in sick and I would be covering the night tour. As I waited for the car the lieutenant on the ladder company was telling me over a cup of coffee that both companies would be out shoveling hydrants. Each company has a pre-arranged hydrant district. Both the ladder and the engine were riding heavy, each with two extra men. As the night's events unfolded, they were definitely needed.

We were driving down Massachusetts Avenue in Central Square when the alert tone sounded on the radio. "Striking box three nine two one for a building fire on Magazine Street near the corner of Upton Street." Fire Alarm then called me: "Fire alarm calling C Two. We are receiving numerous calls on this box for a fire in a rooming house on Magazine Street." I was acknowledging the call when Jerry turned onto Magazine Street. The sight before me was a script for a firefighter's horror show. The involved building was a large, wood frame, two and a half story dwelling. Heavy fire was overlapping from four or five first floor windows on the Magazine Street side, and people on the second floor were jumping out the windows into the snow.

I did not hesitate. "C Two to Fire Alarm."

"Answering, C Two."

"On the orders of Acting Deputy Chief O'Brien, strike a second alarm and give me an additional ladder company."

I was now out of the car and on the portable radio. Ladders 3 was about four blocks away shoveling hydrants and were doing their best to get clear and respond. Engine 2 pulled right in behind me. The pump located at a hydrant at the corner of Upton and Magazine. When the pump operator went to open the dammed hydrant it fell over. A plow or something had hit it. Now Engine 2 had only the water carried in the hose wagon, but it would take a great deal more than that to knock this fire down. Firefighters are trained to think on their feet. When Engine 6, approaching from another direction, heard that Engine 2 had a problem, they automatically laid a couple of two

—153—

and a half inch feeder lines into Two's pump. Wading through waist high snow I reached the rear of the building. Heavy fire was now blowing out the second and third floor windows seriously exposing the adjacent dwelling. Ladder 1 had arrived and members were taking people out the windows on the second floor. Ladder 3 was soon at the scene and removing people over ladders on the Magazine Street side. Naturally, the deep snow made ladder work extremely difficult. The area also had an eerie darkness because of the loss of power in the district.

I was standing near the front door when I felt a tugging at my coat. I turned to my left and found a horribly burned person standing next to me—sizzling in the snow. Most of the clothes were burnt off. It was a sight that I will long remember. He spoke to me in a pleading voice, saying, "Please, mister, will you help me? I'm burning." He was still actually burning. Once you have smelled the sickly sweet pungent odor of burnt human flesh, you remember it forever. As I laid the poor man down in the snow his skin came off in my glove. Captain Caldwell of the Rescue Company was there and the victim was taken to the hospital.

In all, four persons jumped and five were rescued over ladders. The jumpers landed in snowbanks and were not seriously injured. Engine companies moved in and all exposures were quickly covered. The fire was knocked down and the involved areas were overhauled. I had just declared it under control when another box was struck for a dwelling fire about four miles away. The Division 3 deputy responded and it also went to two alarms. It was later determined that both fires were the direct result of the storm. Due to the power failures in the area, candles had been used to provide light. Any type of open flame should never be left unattended. A small flickering candle can, under proper circumstance, become a raging inferno and can take a life.

THE EAST BOSTON FIRES

Usually when we covered Boston's Engine 10 in the Beacon Hill section of Boston, we didn't move out of their district. However, this time was to be an exception. We had just backed in and reported to Boston that we were in quarters when we were dispatched to respond to the five alarm fire in East Boston. All that I really knew about the fire was that it involved a block of taxpayer type occupancies with dwellings over. This section of Boston is northeast of the city; it is not actually connected to the city. In order to get there it is necessary to go through the Sumner Tunnel which runs under Boston harbor. East Boston consists of a large residential section with countless attached, wooden, three story dwellings, a small commercial center, but a sizable waterfront with many decaying piers. Years ago the great steamship companies were located there, but today much of the waterfront area is vacant and poses a very real fire danger.

When we arrived at the fire I could see that it was of major proportions. Apparently the fire had started in the rear first floor of an unused department store and had communicated to adjacent stores and also to a large meeting hall above. The weather was cold and windy with a temperature of about ten degrees above zero. A brisk wind was blowing in from the harbor further complicating operations. Heavy fire was showing from the roof of the stores and blowing out the windows of the meeting hall. The chief to whom I reported ordered me to lay a feeder line to a pump that needed additional water. Engine 21 was connected to a hydrant on Summer Street and was drawing a vacuum. We laid two lines of two and a half into Twenty One and their residual pressure went up. They were supplying lines to deck guns and a ladder pipe. We had just finished connecting the lines when a chief ordered us to relieve companies working on the third floor. We followed the lines up the front stairs. The smoke on the second floor was starting to get heavy. Depending on how much work you were doing, our Scott 4.5 masks air supply could last about twenty five minutes. If you were breathing fast, you would go through an air bottle in less time. When the air supply is exhausted, an alarm bell sounds warning you to get out of the building. You must start your exit then. To run out of air can mean suffocation.

Hot water was cascading down the stairs. A company was pulling ceilings on the second floor. I also heard the sound of breaking glass somewhere above us. At the head of the stairs on the third floor a district chief met us. He told us to relieve the company standing by as the truckies opened up. They had been up there for a while and were glad to take a blow. Up to that time the visibility had been good. The smoke was at ceiling level. Fire was now showing in the ceiling. Suddenly visibility went to zero. The entire ceiling in the hallway between us and the stairs that we had used to enter the third floor had collapsed.

We didn't know it at the time but the falling debris had caught the men who had just left us. Flame was now rolling along the entire hallway. The heat was terrific! We still had the pipe and held it over our heads. The boiling hot water was cascading down on top of us. We were trapped! The exit toward the stairs was an inferno and the air regulators of our masks were clicking furiously, indicating that our fifteen minute air supply was rapidly being used up. Debris covered the line making it impossible to move. We had nowhere to go but down the hallway. I could feel the panic rising within me. When you panic, you breathe faster, thus using more air. I could hear Bobby saying, "Oh Jesus! Oh Jesus!" over and over through his mask. Charlie was trying to move the hose line. Visibility was still zero. More sections of the ceiling were coming down behind us. Leaving the line we started to crawl down the hall away from the intense heat. It was a strange feeling doing what you were trained never to do—leave the line! The men had grabbed the belts of the man in front. Now the problem was where the hell are we and how do we get out? The wall that I had been following was ending, turning left. Bobby and Charlie were right on my heels. The voice inside my head is saying, Don't panic! Don't panic! I was trying to decide if we should go left and follow the wall or go straight and hope for the best when I heard more breaking glass in front of me, then I could see it, a glimmer of light. We were headed toward a window. The boys were still behind me and the fire was not far behind them. It sounded like a freight train. I could see a jake in the window cleaning out the glass. God bless him! He's saved our lives. He had a startled look on his unmasked face when he saw us: "Where the fuck did you guys come from?"

    Out on the fire escape we pulled our face masks off. The fresh air sure felt wonderful, like a gift from God. An engine company was advancing a big line up the steel stairs toward us. The officer said, "Get the hell out of here and take a blow!" Out on the street I noted that my knees felt a little wobbly. Charlie was a little pale. Bobby wanted a dry cigarette. We sat on the running board of a ladder truck and smoked in silence. There was nothing to say. We had made it out and that was that. Later I heard that the crew we relieved just made the stairs in time when all hell broke loose. They had called May Day and reported that we were up there and possibly trapped. Now the entire third floor was a sea of flame. The fire was now seven alarms. Someone told us where the coffee wagon was and we headed in that direction. The coffee sure tasted good! Master streams were now in use and all fire-fighting personnel were ordered out of the building. The attack would now be exterior only. The building was coming apart. I reported to the command center and was told to go into a store and warm up.

The store was crowded with jakes with smoke streaked faces. They were sitting on the floor and counter. Charlie said he didn't feel well. We laid him down on the floor and unhooked his rubber coat. He looked really pale. After the EMTs gave him some oxygen, he said that he felt better but sleepy. This could be an indication of carbon monoxide poisoning. The EMTs transported him to Boston City Hospital. He was held overnight and released the next day.

The fire was finally knocked down and we were told to return to cover Engine 10. We had lost six lengths of hose plus a playpipe in the fire. Boston would replace them later. There was no one covering Ten when we got there. We used dry hose from Engine 10's hose rack to repack the wagon. I went up to the office and sat in the easy chair. Close only counts in the game of horseshoes. We had come close, but our wings were not singed and we would fly again.

Baby Doll

It was one of those steamy, hot nights when you wait for something to happen. We didn't have to wait long. The usual false alarms had occurred. I was standing out in front of Engine 2 and Ladder 3 when a car drove up onto the ramp. Even before I could see them I could hear them. A middle-aged woman was in the driver's seat. Sitting next to her was a little man who looked about the same age. She was screaming at the man. He just sat there, not saying a word. Maybe that was just as well because he wouldn't have been able to get a word in edgewise.

Now she was out of the car and yelling for him to stay where he was. We just stood there as she approached. She looked like a housewife who had just been short changed at the local supermarket. She brushed back the hair that was partly covering her face and spoke to us in a voice that, even though she was trying hard, could not conceal her anger. "I have something in the trunk of this dammed car that you boys can use," she said scornfully. She walked to the back of the car and opened the trunk. Out popped a rather large rubber doll. It was a sex doll. The kind that you blow up. Now the story enfolded.

She had gone to her usual Saturday afternoon card party but had left the game early. Upon returning home she had found lover boy in bed with his inflated lady. She pulled the doll from the trunk of the car and handed it to Joe.

"Ma'am, why do you think we need something like this?" I

asked.

"You guys have to spend long hours in that firehouse," she responded, "maybe you can make use of it. My grandfather was a fireman and he never was home much."

"Well, thank you just the same, ma'am, but we have no use for the little rubber lady," I told her.

After stuffing the doll with the funny smile back into the trunk she drove off. Joe then said to me, "Ya know, Captain, if she played her cards right, maybe he wouldn't've fell in love with the doll."

"Well, Joe," I said, "I honestly hope we'll never know."

The Vendome

The day was June 17, 1972. It was to be a warm day, partly cloudy and humid. I had finished my coffee. The firehouse was not the ideal place to be. It would be much better to pack the kids into the car and head for Lake Walden. Peggy would fill the wading pool in the backyard and this would keep the kids happy for the afternoon. Maybe when I got home from work we'd go for a ride and get ice cream. Engine 7 was a pretty good duty station. It was certainly better than floating from one station to another. One drawback was that there was no kitchen in Engine 7. There never had been one. Most of the guys carried a lunch or picked up a sandwich at the Tek Restaurant across the street from the station.

Tuesday was in-service inspection day; we would be going out in the afternoon. Being a new captain in a station required a period of adjustment. There were new officers and company members. I found that the easiest course to follow was to make changes slowly. My plan was simple: initially I would just observe the way the company operated. My predecessor was a competent fire officer and had a good working company. It would not be necessary to make any radical changes.

Lunch was over and we were getting ready to go out on inspections. I was standing in front of the station when I heard the Rescue coming down Main Street. Usually when they headed toward the Charles River we would be involved. It could be any type of incident—a jumper off the bridge, an accident along Memorial Drive, a car in the Charles River, or someone under the train that crossed the bridge into Boston. As it turned out it was none of these things. Walter Long was the lieutenant on the Rescue and he never failed to wave at us as they passed. He would be waving for us to follow them and then the phone would ring telling us to respond with the Rescue. This time, however, the phone remained silent. I remember shrugging my shoulders and thinking it odd that they didn't need us.

Curiosity soon got the best of me and I called Fire Alarm. The operator did not give me a chance to say much and he was obviously very busy. "Engine Seven, cover Boston Engine Ten." I acknowledged. It took about four minutes to cross over the West Boston Bridge to Beacon Hill to Ten's quarters. After we backed in I called Boston Fire Alarm to tell them we were there. The response was quick: "OK, Cam-bridge, you're at Engine Ten." At this point I didn't know what the hell was going on. There obviously was a fire somewhere, but what was burning? The Beacon Hill section of Boston is a maze of narrow one way streets surrounding the State House. Firefighting there can be a be a horror show. If you take the wrong turn up the hill you're done. The houses are attached row style and for the most part second class, brick and wood construction. Due to the hills ladder work can be tricky.

The first indication we got that tragedy had struck was when an off duty member came into quarters and told us that at least nine firefighters were missing at a fire on Commonwealth Avenue. "There was a structural collapse," he concluded and he was out the door. Other jakes came in, got their gear and were gone. I do recall the look on their faces. It was one of shock and pain. We were all in shock. Every firefighter who pulls on a helmet knows well in his or her heart the true danger of the job. This is the reason you give an extra tight hug to those you love when you leave for work. It could well be the last expression of love they will get from you.

The fire was in a former hotel that was under renovation. The heavy fire had essentially been knocked down and companies were overhauling. Fresh crews were relieving companies. Without warning an entire section of the structure collapsed. Some members were killed instantly, others were trapped under tons of red hot brick. Without fear of subsequent collapse, fellow firefighters were digging in the debris with their bare hands to get to their trapped brothers. Extra heavy rescue units were dispatched to the scene. All this time the entire weakened structure could have collapsed at any moment. Members of the clergy were there. One by one those who had fallen were located. There is a tradition among us that the members of a fallen brother's company remove his body; and this was done. A silence fell over the men as the bodies were removed. With bowed head they held their helmets to their breast. In each heart was the realization that, but for being in the right place at the right time, it could be any one of them. When the members returned to Engine 10, their faces told it all. They sat around the kitchen table, each man lost in his own thoughts. One by one they stood up, went to the sink, washed a cup and went home.

The morning of the funeral dawned gray and rainy. Brother and sister firefighters from all points of the compass attended the funeral, including about 175 members of the Cambridge Fire Department. The funeral Mass was said at the Cathedral of the Holy Cross in Boston. The church was packed. Those who could not get inside were lined four abreast outside. A businessman had donated plastic raincoats to the members who stood outside in the rain.

To be a firefighter is to be dedicated to those we serve.

When duty calls, and there is a job to be done, I have never known a firefighter who would hesitate to do what has to be done. It is my firm belief that when the end comes, a voice will say, "Come to me, my good and faithful friend. You have served me well."

BENNY

He sat there looking at me with a confused look on his face. It was a simple question. Where is Otis Street? Tim O'Malley had been transferred to Engine 7 from Engine 4 in North Cambridge and had been on the job for about two years. Now he was clearly in trouble. "Gee, Captain," he replied in a thick Irish brogue, "I do have a problem remembering the names of streets." Engine 7 was located on Main Street in Kendall Square near the West Boston Bridge. I had been assigned there about three months. When you have been transferred into an unfamiliar district, street and box locations can be a bit of a problem. I knew this particular area fairly well because I had lived in the housing project not far from the station.

How could I help Tim to remember streets? After chewing on it for awhile I came up with an idea. All streets ran parallel to Main Street all the way up to Cambridge Street. To respond to box and still alarms in the East Cambridge area, we would normally take Third Street toward Cambridge Street which ran from the Boston line north. This route would take us across Binney, Rodgers, Bent, Charles, Hurley, Spring, Thondike, Otis, Cambridge, and Gore to the Somerville line. After thinking about it a bit, I came up with a story that might help Tim: "There was a Portuguese fellow named Benny Rodgers. He was a very muscular fellow who lifted weights. He had a friend named Charles Hurley who bent a big steel Spring.

Charlie was so impressed that he told another friend whose name was Thorndike Otis. Mister Otis became the richest man in Cambridge. One day poor Mister Otis was hit by a streetcar. It was a Gory mess. He was buried in Somerville." Tim just sat there and stared at me. He was slowly shaking his head.

The next drill day he said, "Hey, Captain, I want to tell you a story about East Cambridge." We were sitting at the table in back of the pump. Engine 7 had no formal kitchen; we had a gas stove and a metal cabinet with some dishes in it. Without any assistance from the paper I had given him, Tim recited the tale perfectly. Tim knew every street all the way up to Gore Street and the Somerville line. Each time we responded up Third Street toward Cambridge Street and he was driving, he would mumble, "Benny, Rodgers, Bent, Charles, Hurley, Spring, Thorndike, Otis, Cambridge, Gore."

Ice Cream

The transfers were out. Usually the rumors would start long before the actual new assignments came out. You were going here...no, you were being shipped there...and he was being shipped here...and the other guy's....Then, finally, a general order would come down from headquarters listing the men to be given new duty assignments.

Transfers are necessary within any department for a variety of reasons—new members being appointed, requests for reassignment, and to maintain the proper workforce balance. Occasionally men would get upset about being sent to another station. For the most part, however, transfers are made for the good of the department and are necessary.

The order usually came out on Sunday, and I was home when I received a call from Lieutenant Roberts that I had been transferred from Engine 2 to captain of Engine 3 in East Cambridge. My first duty day would be the following Monday night tour. Engine 3 is located in the same quarters as Ladder 2. Each company has a captain. I knew the fellow who was in command of Ladder 2 and was confident we'd work well together. Since I was also the senior captain in the division, I would be covering the deputy's car as acting deputy when required. We were working a four group system and a lieutenant would be in charge of the ladder truck.

Every year in the early fall, each engine company inspects

all the hydrants in their district. This is very important because in many cases hydrants have been hit and damaged. When you would go to open one at a fire it would malfunction. This could cause a serious delay in running lines and a fire could get away. Hydrants can also freeze solid if they aren't properly drained after a fire. Threads must be checked to assure that quick connections can be made.

We were due to start hydrant inspection my first tour of duty at Engine 3. It was a beautiful fall evening. The first hydrant to be examined was at Seventh and Spring Streets. The boys would service the hydrant and I would do the necessary paperwork. We had completed about four inspections when I decided that we should take a break. We were only four blocks away from a great ice cream store up on Cambridge Street. I was seated up in the cab of the pump and as I started the engine I yelled to the guys, "Let's take a break and get some ice cream," and off I drove in a cloud of diesel smoke.

Up on Cambridge Street I parked the pump, walked into the store and said "Hello!" to the nice attractive woman behind the counter.

"Good-a evening, sir," she responded in an Italian accent.

"Good evening! I'd like a medium vanilla cone and give the boys," and here I pointed behind me, "whatever they want—on me."

The woman tilted her head a bit and looked at me strangely before speaking: "Yes, sir...you-a...you are going to have-a medium vanilla cone....but...what-a boys are you talkin' about!"

What boys indeed! I turned around and discovered I was alone in the ice cream store. All the boys were back at the hydrant; they hadn't heard me. Then it happened: "Fire Alarm calling Engine Company Three." I acknowledged on the portable. "Respond to a reported building fire on Otis Street."

Oh my! I was two blocks away with an ice cream cone and a fire engine with no crew.

With pounding heart I jumped into the cab and returned to where I left the boys. They were still there, walking up the street towards me with looks of sheer amazement on their faces. Apparently their previous commanding officers had never abandoned them!

"Jump on! Jump on! We've got a fire!" I called, sliding over to the shotgun side of the front seat.

As Larry, the pump operator, slid behind the wheel he said, "That's nice, Captain. Where'd you find the fire?"

The fire turned out to be food burning on the stove. The lady had burned a pot of stew. We returned to hydrant inspection. On the way home from the firehouse the next morning I stopped at the ice cream store to pay for my cone. The same woman was working, and in a fine Italian accent she said to me, "You-a strange man. You find-a you boys?"

"Yes, ma'am, I did," I responded. "They're good boys and they were right where I left them."

LEROY

I first heard that he was coming to Engine 3 through the grapevine. I also heard that he was a real foul ball who would be nothing but trouble. Trouble I did not need and I hoped that it was just another rumor. However, the official notice came a couple of weeks later; Leroy was to be assigned to my company. The order came out the following Wednesday to become effective on Sunday. He was not only assigned to my company, he was assigned to my group. One of my best men was transferred to another company. To say that I was upset would not be telling the full story, but I just shrugged my shoulders and decided I would just have to do my best to try to accept the situation.

He stood there smiling at me, finally saying, "Well, Captain, I guess you're stuck with me." He was a black man, about six foot and built like a Mack truck. I told him to sit down and I closed the office door. I looked straight into his face and replied that I didn't look at it that way. As far as I was concerned a man would have to show me. "Every new man comes into the company with a clean slate," I said. "All I expect is a good day's work."

During the first week that he was with us I noted that he was doing his best to upset the working group. His comments were strictly negative. We had another little talk and I told him that his attitude would do nothing but complicate his life with the group. His smile told me that he had no intentions of changing and becoming a team player.

The alarm of fire came in about 7:15 on a Thursday night for a large Elks Lodge that was under renovation. We were not scheduled to respond on the first alarm. The first engine company to arrive reported heavy smoke showing from the second and third floors. C2 went off at the box and immediately called for a second alarm. Ladder 3 was calling C 2 and reporting heavy fire coming through the roof at the rear of the building.

Leroy had the floor patrol and was on the PA yelling, "We go on the second!" The truck stationed with us was to cover Ladder 1. Even from four blocks away I could see the glow in the sky. C2's aide was now practically screaming that there was fire spreading to wood frame three deckers at the rear of the building. I knew that Larry, the chief's aide, was not prone to panic; I viewed his loud tone as an indication of the situation's severity.

We picked up a hydrant on Broadway and laid a big line to the front of the structure. The Division 2 chief was waiting for us and ordered us to advance into the building and hit the fire on the upper floors. He said that he had companies running lines into guns to handle the rear exposure. He also told us that the bartender was unaccounted for. "Keep an eye out for him," the chief yelled. I had been in the building once or twice and vaguely remembered some type of balcony on the second floor. There was a side entrance and it looked as good as any place to enter.

Most firefighters experience a fleeting sense of concern just before we enter a burning building. Leroy had a look of fear on his face. His hands were fumbling as he attempted to put on his mask. His six foot frame was shuddering. I supposed he wished that he were somewhere—anywhere—else. After opening his air cylinder and adjusting his mask, I asked him if he was ready. He didn't answer me. When I handed him the playpipe, he seemed amazed. My assurance that we were right with him did little to allay his fears. The interior was pitch black and we were at the foot of a stairway. Leroy was holding back. He did not want to go up.

After a few prods he slowly ascended the stairs. At the second floor landing we saw the red devil. Tongues of flame were rolling across the ceiling directly at us. We had water and I told him to hit the flame. Leroy still wanted no part of the action and was moving back down the stairs. "Hit it now!" I commanded. It had to be now or we would have to retreat. We were lying flat on the stairs and my body was partly on top of his. He could not move down! When the pipe was finally opened, the scalding shower started. The cold water was hitting the flame and coming back on us as steam. "Hit it! Hit it!" I yelled. Now my new gallant warrior was not only hitting flame but he was squirming up the stairs.

All the heavy fire in front of us was darkened down. When you're inside working you tend to lose track of time. We were getting low on air and it was time to back down. Also, I didn't like the sounds that I was hearing ahead of us. It sounded like we were in a large room and there was an echo. Later we learned that we were on a balcony and the railing had been removed!

Outside the fresh air felt good. Leroy had me in a bear hug and I feared that he was about to kiss me. "Oh Captain! I saw the red devil and I gave it a lick! Oh Captain, I been there and the devil is down!"

Other guys were looking at us strangely. "Yes, you did fine, Leroy," I repeated over and over as I tried to escape his embrace.

From that moment on Leroy was a changed man. He was

eager to get involved in a positive way. When we had a fire he was first pipe, he really wanted the nozzle. He sat in my office and told me that all his life people had no confidence in him. His father used to beat him until he was senseless. He saw little of his mother. For the most part an aunt raised him in the slums of Boston. He said that all the tricks he learned were necessary to survive.

It was a cold, rainy night and I was sitting at the patrol desk down off the apparatus floor. We had just started our night tour. The ladder and engine crews were up on the third floor. As captain of the engine company it was my job to set up the watch list and cover assignments. Normally the outside door is locked. From the patrol desk anyone ringing the buzzer can be observed through a window. For some reason, however, the door was open on that particular night and I never heard them enter. There were three men and they looked like they meant business. "Leroy Smith working tonight?" one of them asked in a rough, authoritative voice.

My right hand moved to the receiver of the red phone. This line goes directly to Fire Alarm. My left hand was on the desk microphone. These three just didn't look right to me. "Leroy's on vacation," I replied. Even with their heavy raincoats it was obvious to me that they were packing guns.

Again they asked me and again I told them that he was not here. Then there was a silence, as if they were debating whether to believe me or not. Now my hand was on the mike button, and then there were voices out on the apparatus floor, and that seemed to help them make up their minds to leave.

Later that night I asked Leroy to come to the engine office. He listened intently as I related the incident and described the men. He didn't say a word, just stared at me, then he stood up and left the office. About an hour later there was a knock on my door. It was Leroy and he had all his equipment in his arms. He piled all the equipment on the floor in front of my desk—all the equipment that had been issued to him, mask face pieces, helmet, turnout gear, boots, everything. "Well, Captain, I'm quittin' now," he said. To say the least I was amazed. When I asked him what this was all about he replied, "Captain, you're one of the few who believed in me as long as I've been on this job. You showed me the red devil and I beat him. Them men who came here tonight are bad. I don't want you boys to get hurt so I'm gonna quit. I got some people moving in on me and I better move on—fast."

Trying to reason with him was fruitless. He put out his hand, I shook it and he was gone. When I called the division chief and told him about Leroy's abrupt departure, he said that there was no sense chasing after him, to put it all on paper and submit it in the morning.

Through the years I heard that Leroy was here or there but nothing conclusive. We never talked again. Maybe if someone had taken the time to talk to him earlier in his life the rest of his life would have been different. We'll never know.

CAUGHT IN A STORM

The crew and I had sent out for lunch. I had got up a little late and told Peg to forget about packing a lunch. It was a hot and sultry day and neither of us had slept that well. Ladder 3 in the Cambridgeport section of the city was a new experience for me. For most of my career I'd been assigned to engine companies. However, I was a newly promoted captain, and Ladder 3 was the next opening.

The truck was located in the lower section of the city and was considered a busy assignment. We were housed with Engine Company 2. The house was divided into the engine and ladder sides, and they had their own captains, lieutenants and crews. The engine was a two piece company—a pumper and a hose wagon. We usually cleared the house before them. At a fire we worked closely together.

It was one in the afternoon and I was working on some reports I had to prepare, but the bed looked so inviting and I was seriously thinking about a little nap when the phone rang down at the patrol desk. The intercom crackled to life: "Still alarm. Ladder Three to the First Baptist Church at Western Ave. and Massachusetts Ave." As we turned left up Mass. Ave. I noted that the sky to the west was a dirty gray. The weather forecaster during the "News at Noon" had predicted heavy thunderstorms headed towards the metropolitan area.

Three police cars were waiting for us. A young sergeant came over to inform me that there was a jumper up in the staging of the church. This church is located in the center of Central Square and is one of the largest edifices in the city. The steeple was undergoing much needed repairs. Pipe staging extended from the ground to the top, about 175 feet. The rumble of thunder was closer now and that leaden gray sky was jet black. The sergeant told me that the jumper was a young fellow who had been fired from his job, and then his wife threw him out. The police had talked to him when he wasn't too high up in the scaffolding, but when they tried to get near him he only climbed higher.

Now it was raining. We were in for a bad storm. Larry grabbed a 150 foot life line and we all put on Pompier belts. The Pompier has a large safety hook that could be attached to the pipe staging. The sexton of the church agreed to lead us to a window the steeplejacks used to get to the staging.

The interior wooden stairs led us to a narrow open window about fifty feet from the ground. Outside the rain was getting harder. As I stepped out onto the aluminum catwalk I noted that the wind was causing the staging to sway. The climber was about another thirty feet above me. We did not make eye contact. As soon as he saw me he started to climb higher. I stepped on the railing and started up after him. Larry was right behind me. Now the wind was really moving the staging. I could hear the pipes twisting in the wind. This is ridiculous, I thought. If only the son of a bitch would stop so I could talk to him. Just then he stopped and leaned over the edge, shaking the staging. Larry yelled at him, "You silly bastard, *jump* so we all can go home!" It didn't seem such a bad idea.

I remembered reading somewhere that jumpers who yell may not jump. Now all hell was breaking loose. Thunder and lightning were right over us. He was finally making eye contact with me, and I said in a pleading voice, "You know, buddy, we can't leave here until you come down. Give us a break. This dammed thing is starting to come apart and we all could be history. As far as I'm concerned, my kids would like to see their father again. Tell you what, let's all get to hell off this thing and get a cup of coffee." My plea was falling on deaf ears and I knew it.

Larry had climbed down a little way and was yelling over the howling wind, "Fuck him! Jump, you crazy bastard."

I looked back up at him and I was amazed to see him climbing down after me. It was different this time; he was descending carefully. The police were waiting for us at the window and placed him under arrest. As he passed me I said, "Thanks." He had a half smile on his face. The storm was passing and the wind had slacked off.

Back in the station we had a cup of coffee and I headed upstairs to do reports. Leaning back in the chair I thought to myself, What a crazy job this is! After all these years, this is still a *crazy* job!

CAN YOU PLAY THE SPOONS?

The Local 30 union meeting had taken longer than expected. Important issues were coming in the near future and they needed to be discussed, but sometimes the discussions and debates seemed to go on and on with little solved. By the time we finished we needed a beer. Dan and I left the hall and decided we'd head to Dailey's Pub in downtown Boston. Wednesday nights were usu-ally slow, so we figured it wouldn't be crowded.

Dailey's is a really Irish pub and on Wednesday night they usually hosted a séisun, an informal gathering of amateur and professional musicians who will play Irish songs on various traditional Irish instruments. Perhaps a fiddler will start, then as the musicians arrive they will join in with their own contribution to the sound. There might be a fiddle, a banjo, a bodrun drum, guitars, another fiddle, and maybe a flute or two, a pipe and, of course, a tin whistle. All in all the sound would be great!

We were sitting at the bar enjoying our beer when Danny spotted someone he knew sitting in the other side of the room. Dan went across the room talking to his friend and I sat at the bar, tapping my feet on the bar rail. There were now about eight musicians sitting in a circle and I was really enjoying the music. A petite waitress came to me and asked with a lilting Irish accent, "Can you play the spoons?" I replied that with one more beer I would be able to play the Irish Anthem on the spoons. Soon my little lass provided me with two soup spoons saying, "Da, join in the fun." Her broad smile told me that I was welcome.

Now the music was reaching a new crescendo. My spoons were beating a melodic click as they ricocheted off my knee. Soon, under my guiding hand, they were bouncing off the oak bar. A young lady was now singing in Gaelic. She swayed back and forth to the rhythm of the drum and her voice blended with the clicking of my spoons. The young lady playing the drum was rocking gently back and forth. The fellow playing lead fiddle glanced at me and gave his nod of approval. That was all that I needed. Now my spoons were flying with unabashed abandon. The little waitress who gave me the spoons was doing a step dance to the music. Someone set me up for an another beer.

Dan's friend, a young Irish lad, was also playing the spoons. He was using the wrist method. When the set ended Dan called me over to their table: "Connie, you've been playing the spoons all wrong! Watch Shamus." Shamus, indeed, was a better spoon player than I. He was using two hands and four spoons. There was also someone else watching him—the fiddle player. He was not smiling at all. In fact he had a frown on his face. Shamus gave me a quick conversion lesson on the proper method of making spoon music.

Soon the music started again. First one player then another would join in. Shamus also began to play with his spoons. Now I joined in and was quick to adjust to his method. When I glanced over at the lead fiddler it was very obvious that something was amiss. The music stopped and a waiter snatched our spoons away as he wiped the table. The look of astonishment on the Irish lad's face could not be described. "Hey boy, what the hell are you doing?"

The waiter, in a voice dripping with apology, said, "Eamon, the fiddle player, says you're were out of tune."

The young Shamus immediately removed his scally cap, stood up and flung it violently on the floor. "I have never been insulted like this in my life."

The waiter was now placing a full pitcher of beer on the table, saying in hushed tones that the beer was compliments of the house. I had little to say, thinking that perhaps my lack of agility with the spoons caused the ruckus.

With a sweeping motion my new fellow musician knocked the full picture to the floor. "You tell the fiddler that I want more satisfaction than that." What a pity as I was just about to pour myself a fresh glass of sparkling brew!

Two Irish girls were sitting with Shamus and they were urging him on. Now Shamus was in a fighting stance and ready to go. I was thinking that Dan and I should be thinking about going also. Dan was no help at all—he was laughing so hard that he nearly fell on the floor with the beer.

The big burly manager was now telling us that we were no longer welcome. Dan was now in convulsions. Yes, it was time to leave. Someone on the other side of the bar shouted that the police were here. Now we'd be playing spoons in jail. The waitress slipped on the wet floor and fell down. Shamus was trying to get at the fiddler. I was smiling at the police. Dan was still enjoying his laugh. The two greenhorn ladies were making a point to the police officers. One cop in a thick brogue was saying, "Let's all calm down now!" Peace was returning to Dailey's Pub.

Shamus, Dan, and I were ejected from the premises. The two ladies were also asked to leave. One of the colleens said to me, "Come on, Da! We can all go to a pub in Brighton where you can play the spoons till dawn." Da had had enough. My career as a traditional Irish musician was over.

A Dash of Radiation

The fire service changed dramatically during the years I was on the job. Gone are the old style smoke eaters. When I started out, I think we all believed we could actually breathe smoke. At the time we didn't realize that we were just as vulnerable as any other firefighter. For example, behind the driver's seat of the hose wagon was a box containing an MSA mask. However, to reach for it and put it on was similar to admitting that you were a coward. Apparently, the marks of a true firefighter were the length of the mucus that hung from his nose and how bloodshot his eyes were.

Like many old East Coast cities, Cambridge is a densely populated municipality that has good chunks of its real estate devoted to industry and manufacturing. However, Cambridge is also unique because of its concentration of cutting edge research and development operations that are conducted at Harvard University and MIT or at commercial spin-offs of these academic institutions. Cambridge is noted all over the world as a center for all types of chemical and nuclear research. Almost daily firefighters are expected to expose themselves to some form of experimental hazard. Often these incidents occur during the night when few of the "acknowledged experts" are available to tell you exactly what is going on and exactly what you are dealing with.

I especially remember a fire that occurred near MIT during the time I was captain of Engine 2. We had a smokey fire in the ceiling of a former factory building that, among other things, had been used for processing uranium. The fire was difficult because it was spreading above the sprinklers. We were playing catch-up and losing badly. Once a fire gets into void spaces above the ceiling you have big trouble. The fire was on the third floor, and what had once been wide open floor space had been divided into numerous offices. It was a maze up there. Each office was locked and required forcible entry. The problem in this type of renovation is that the ceiling has been dropped and altered many times. The void area over the suspended ceiling provides a near perfect flue for fire to spread. Each time we thought we had it someone would yell that they had fire in the ceiling ahead of us. It was a rainy night and the smoke just wouldn't lift. The smoke had now banked down to knee level.

A ladder company was with us and was forcing the office doors open. The lieutenant of the ladder company reported to me that there were "Danger—Radiation" symbols on the office doors. I passed on this information to the command chief. When not in use, radiation material is kept locked in a lead container. However, the fire can cause structural alteration that can move the containers from their place of safety and smash them onto a floor below.

We were finally able to get ahead of the fire. It required a lot of pulling of ceilings to expose the fire traveling in concealed spaces. The ladder companies set up smoke ejectors to get rid of the smoke. The chief kept one engine and one ladder company for overhaul and told us to return to quarters.

While the boys repacked the hose wagon with dry hose, I went up to the office to fill out a fire report. About an hour after we returned I received a phone call from the deputy who had been in charge of the fire. He informed me that the entire crew had to be tested for possible radiation poisoning! To say the least this was unnerving. We would be placed out of service and all the clothing we wore while working at the fire was to be kept in a separate pile. This included all protective gear. We were also instructed to take showers and to use plenty of soap. Hmmmm!

After we showered and put on fresh clothes, we were transported to the Cambridge City Hospital in two MIT police cruisers. Chest x-rays and blood tests were taken...and then we waited. Every time I asked someone what the hell was going on we were told we would have to wait. It was now 7:00 a.m. and worrying wives would be looking for us to come home. I didn't want Fire Alarm to call Peggy; their call would alarm her. There were only two pay phones in the emergency room lobby. We took turns calling home. There were nine of us between Ladder 2 and Engine 3, and twenty seven men in all.

You can imagine the scenarios of horror that were going through our minds. Harry Leach wondered if he would glow at night. Finally, a doctor told us that we were OK and could go home. However, if we noticed any change in our general health we were to contact MIT. When I arrived home I was actually afraid to hug my wife and kids. What a strange, strange job!

A Twinkle in his Eye

Now there was no question about it. The police car was following him. Now it was right on his tail and the blinking blue light on the roof was telling him to pull over to the curb. He had left the firehouse an hour ago. The only stop he'd made was at Verna's for a cup of coffee.

He had worked last night and it had been one of those tours. They had been in and out all night and had one job, a mattress fire at 3:45 a.m. In short, it had been a lousy night. There were reports to fill out and by the time he had finished, out they went. This time it was an automobile accident. The driver had fallen asleep at the wheel and the car had then hit a parked vehicle.

He had pulled over to the side of the road. The cruiser was parked right on his tail. Bill smiled at the young officer.

"License and registration, please," the police officer said.

Bill complied with the request. "What's the trouble officer?" he asked.

"The trouble is you were doing sixty miles an hour in a forty mile zone."

Bill thought, Boy, does he look mad! "Gee, officer, if I may explain...you see I'm a Cambridge firefighter and we had a very busy night."

The officer was not paying much attention to Bill as he continued to write.

"You see, officer, we had a bad fire and I was trying to blow the smoke out of my eyes."

The officer stopped writing, raised his head and stared at Bill. "You know my brother in law is a fireman and I bet he has the same line you have. You guys're all cut from the same cloth."

Now the police officer had a smile on his face.

"On your way—and wash out your eyes when you get home."

"Thanks, officer, I will...and have a Merry Christmas!"

As Bill drove off he said to himself, "Geez, I wonder if he really believed me!"

A Room Full of Candles

Engine 9 went off with smoke showing. The fire was in a complex of two story, frame duplex, second class dwellings off Mount Auburn Street. Chief O'Donnell had called me the last day I worked on Ladder 3 and asked me to cover the Division 2 car tonight as he was going to a party. In Cambridge captains usually covered for a deputy chief. We were on Walden Street when the box was received and John, the chief's aide, said, "that's for us, Connie." As we turned into the complex I could see the smoke curling from under the gutter line of the roof. Engine 9 was running a line into the front door. It was quarter past seven in the evening and most occupants were up. The officer reported to me by radio that it was a small fire in some rubbish. The people had just moved in and had not too wisely placed paper boxes on top of the gas stove. The pilot light of the stove did the rest. Ladder 4 provided ventilation and checked for extension.

I was standing outside in front of the building when one of the guys from Engine 8 asked me to take a look at the first floor of the adjoining apartment. At first I did not know what the hell I was looking at. A large rug or mat was on the parlor floor. Arranged in a circle were about eight cushions, and in front of each cushion was a lit candle. I removed my helmet and started to scratch my head saying, "What the hell is going on here?" Now the men were pointing to objects on the floor. There were long cylinders with rounded heads and other queer objects. All lights in the room were draped with red netting. At first I thought some form of ceremony for some small, strange religious sect or cult was going on. This apartment was separated from the fire by a partition wall that divided it from the other apartment.

A large woman wearing a housecoat came into the room and wanted to know why we were in there. The lieutenant of Engine 8 was trying to explain that they were checking for extension of fire into the apartment. She insisted that we had no business in the apartment and should get out immediately. She was yelling at the lieuten-ant. I reminded the woman that as long as we were at the scene we were entitled to enter in the performance of our duty. Now three or four other women entered the room and joined in the argument; they started calling us "male pigs". I began to think that perhaps retreat was the better part of valor, so I asked the officer of Engine 8 if he was satisfied that there was no extension of fire. He said that the walls were cool.

The companies were making up when a police officer and a detective came up to me and said the occupants of the candle lit apartment were going to the station to lodge a complaint against us. Now I saw red and it was not fire. I notified Fire Alarm to have the arson squad respond to the scene. Inspector Foley was advised of the situation when he arrived. He entered the candle lit apartment and informed the occupants who he was and what he wanted. The large lady wanted to see his badge. He went on to say that in the presence of a police officer each occupant would be interviewed as to where he or she was and what he or she was doing immediately before the fire. The large woman told him that it was none of his business. He said, "Lady, you talk here or down at the station. Which will it be?" She backed down. Now he asked her who was in the room prior to the fire. Next he asked her why the candles were lit on the combustible rug. Again he asked her what was going on. The woman's face was turning red green, pale yellow and reddish blue. She was wringing her hands. The other players were whimpering with embarrassment. The large woman's head was down and I heard her say, "We were just...gathered here...we did not start the fire."

Enough is enough, I thought. I asked Inspector Foley if he had finished. He nodded his head. All lines were made up and I asked for the all out on the box. No police report was ever filed against us. It takes all kinds to make a world. Or at least the city of Cambridge!

Jesse

During the late 80s I was assigned as acting deputy to cover vacations. On this particular night I was covering the Division 1 car. We had just backed into Engine 5's quarters. Usually Thursday would be a slow night. We'd have a few false alarms early, then it would settle down. Engine 5 was my old home and it was nice to get back there once in a while. Jesse Anders was acting lieutenant of Engine 2 that night. I had worked with him when I was the captain there. He was the kind of guy who was a comic and didn't realize it. If there was trouble around, he would be involved. Sitting next to him over a cup of coffee and hearing the latest news from his own personal "Lake Woe Be Gone" was an experience in itself.

One day I asked Jesse how things were at home. He replied that living in a trailer was not as bad as he'd feared. We were amazed! "What the hell happened?" I asked. He coolly replied that things were better since the fire. "What fire?" Things were getting more interesting by the moment. He then told us that his home in Stoneham had burned down. No one at the firehouse knew about it! He then told us that he had also lost his car—which explained the reason he was seen pedaling to work on a bicycle. Jesse was a guy who kept his cards really close to his vest! The guys got together and arranged a committee to find out what the family needed.

On this night I found a note on the deputy's desk; the note

stated that Engine 2 was having a problem with the apparatus door. After coffee we would take a ride down to Two and have a look. It might be necessary to call in an outside service company to make some repairs. The front office, for the most part, frowned on this move. Apparatus doors have always been a big problem. They have been knocked completely off their hinges, and I always said that if they could cry they would do so. I have been personally responsible for knocking down a few. This can be a real problem during the winter months. Salvage covers must be used to cover the doors, and this can be a very drafty, very cold situation. After a door was badly damaged, it could take quite a length of time to get it repaired. This was sometimes the front office's way of saying, "Be more careful, boys!"

We never reached Engine 2. As we passed Hampshire and Columbia Streets, Fire Alarm was announcing a building fire on Massachusetts Avenue. Billy turned right onto Columbia Street, and in the distance I could see Engine 2 and Ladder 3 pulling out.

"Fire Alarm calling C Two."

"C Two answering," I said.

"Chief, we are receiving calls for a fire in the YMCA."

I acknowledged and we turned onto Mass. Ave. Ladder 3 reported off with heavy smoke showing from an upper floor. The traffic in Central Square was not too bad for this time of night, and we were on the scene within minutes. Mass. Ave. is a main drag between Boston and points north and has a well deserved reputation for very heavy traffic. A backup was already starting. Pulling my coat on as I left the car, I told Billy to call the police to handle traffic. This building is six stories high in the front and even higher in the rear. The front is located on Mass. Ave. and the right side extended for one block down hill on Bay Street. The left exposure is attached mercantile occupancies, which are three stories high. The building is used as a men's hotel. We'd had a number of fires in the building. Fortunately, we were able to control them before they spread.

Ladder 1, in the rear of the building, was calling me and reporting that smoke was showing from two windows in the rear. They had gone down Bay Street to the rear of the building on Green Street. It looked like a one room fire, but sometimes looks are deceiving. Engine 5 ran a big line up the front stairs and Engine 1 backed them up. The captain of Ladder 3 called me and reported that there was a heavy smoke condition on the sixth floor. This building was occupied and there was a potential life hazard. I notified Fire Alarm of the extent of the fire and I requested a working fire signal be sounded. I ordered Engine 2 to advance a big line over Ladder 3's aerial and into the sixth floor. Engine 1 was the working fire company and I ordered them to stand ready.

My friend Jesse had a problem. When he stepped into the window on the fire floor from the aerial ladder, his leg somehow got wedged between the windowsill and the radiator. The weight of the hose line and playpipe caused him to lose his balance and he fell forward into the room. His leg was broken. The man behind him, Jack Chenille, was able to extract his leg from behind the radiator. Looking up to the window from the street, I could tell that something was wrong. The main body of fire was in the adjoining room from where Jesse had tried to enter. Companies were moving down the corridor and hitting the fire. Jack Chenille used Jesse's radio to tell me what had happened. Then Captain Norris of Ladder 3 reported that they were in the room and were attending to Jesse. He also reported that the fire was knocked down.

I made my way to the room where Jesse was lying on a bed. His leg was positioned at an awkward angle and his face was flushed with pain as he looked up at me and said, "Hi, Cap." I then told him that we had both good news and bad news. "Gimme the bad news first, Cap."

"Well, Jesse, the main fire is right next door and headed this way," I said. "The good news is that we may be able to save you."

His face relaxed a bit, he gave me that special look and said, "Thanks, Cap."

The fire was extinguished and the room was overhauled. The Rescue Company removed Jesse to the city hospital where his leg was set. It was a compound fracture below the knee. They kept him in the hospital for three days.

I visited him while he was in the hospital. When I entered his room, he had a big basket of fruit on the bed and he was eating a banana. His leg was in traction.

"Hey, Jesse, you look like a monkey swinging from a tree!" I laughed.

"Very funny, Cap! Has your monkey got a broken leg too?"

A Fish Story

Every Christmas the guys and gals would get together and hold a party. The Cambridge FD has four working groups. Groups One and Two would get together, and later Three and Four would have their fling. Tonight it was One and Two. They had rented the veterans' hall in North Cambridge. I was working as acting deputy chief in Group One. We were finishing a cup of coffee at Ladder 2, killing time before we picked up the night chief. The day had been on the dull side. A light rain had been falling for most of the day. Still, with only two weeks until Christmas, people were busy running here and there trying to finish their shopping.

Tonight would be my night to howl. All the gang would be there. We would have dinner and drink a little beer. A good number of the retired guys had said they planned on showing up and it would be wonderful to see them.

The alarm tone sounded, striking box 1265 for a building fire on Fulkerson Street. We hit the pole and headed up Cambridge Street. The traffic was just picking up. Engine 5 from Inman Square would be first due.

"Fire Alarm calling C Two."

"C Two answering," I responded.

"We are receiving calls on this."

I acknowledged and then heard, "Engine Five to Fire Alarm."

"Fire Alarm answering."

"We're on Fulkerson street with heavy fire showing from the fourth floor windows of a six story frame duplex."

Fire Alarm acknowledged.

Even before I got out of the car I called a working fire. A frantic woman ran up to me, yelling that there was an invalid on the fifth floor. As the companies hustled lines I took a walk to the rear of the building. Heavy smoke prevented me from seeing above the third floor. "C Two calling Fire alarm." As soon as they answered me I said, "On the orders of Acting Deputy Chief O'Brien, strike a second alarm."

The fire was now blowing out the windows big time. The lieutenant of the Rescue Company reported to me and I told him to conduct a search for the trapped man. Many times people will become excited and report people missing who have actually already escaped from the fire. Regardless, we make it a practice to conduct a primary and secondary search. Engine 5 advanced a big line up the front stairs backed up by Engine 3. Ladder 2 was on the roof opening up. Rescue reported to me that the primary search was negative. Just about then the woman who had reported the invalid on the fifth floor pointed to him across the street. Second alarm companies were now at the scene and going to work. Once the life hazard was taken care of, the knockdown was routine.

I was on the fifth floor when the captain of Ladder 4 called me by radio and asked to see me. He showed me a potential problem. When they opened the walls to check for hidden fire they discovered that ground paper had been used for insulation. Fire in this type of insulation material is very difficult to extinguish; it would smolder undetected. I told Jimmy that another ladder company would be sent up to help out. A little later the captain of Ladder 4 reported to me that the fire was out and we were in good shape. I went with him to the fire floor and checked around. There was no sign of heat or smoke. Little did I know that the red devil was hiding within the walls.

I was standing outside the building when a man walked up to me. He said that he had expensive, rare tropical fish in his apartment and he wanted to check on them. I consented to take him up there and check out his fish, and when we reached the apartment he was happy to find that the fish were fine. They must have been hungry because he sprinkled some fish food into the tank. Little did I know that it would be their last meal! He wanted to take the more expensive fish with him in a plastic bag, but I assured him that this would not be at all necessary; he would be able to be with his beloved fish tomorrow. If I had only known that, for the fish, tomorrow would never come. He also had some expensive cups and saucers. He was assured he could get them in the morning.

Fire Alarm was notified to contact the boarding up company. Before they arrived I went to the fire floor and checked for myself that the fire was out. It was near relief time and the night shift would be in quarters. The all out was ordered and I went to pick up the night deputy chief. It was nearly party time.

When I arrived at home the house was in darkness. Peggy had been gone for a while and being alone in the house still bothered me. First I wanted to take a nice shower and shave. It would be good to get the smell of smoke off me. My fire radio was on the kitchen table. Then I heard it: "Striking box one two six five for a building fire on Fulkerson Street." My mouth fell open and I got a weak feeling in my knees. No, it couldn't be. The deputy acknowledged and then was told that the involved structure was the same building I had earlier.

Engine 5 again went off with heavy fire showing. This time, though, the fire was through the roof. Yes, it was the worst case scenario. The fire in the walls had rekindled and now the whole dammed place was going.

"C Two calling Fire Alarm."

"Fire alarm answering."

"C Two is at the fire. Strike a second alarm."

My heart sank. There was nothing left to do, so I decided to attend the party. As I drove down to the function hall I had a feeling that some how I had failed. I should have kept a detail company at the scene. Or maybe...maybe it was another fire.

The party had already started when I arrived. Most of the guys were at the bar, and someone handed me a beer. The conversation was not on the fire, but on why the New England Patriots football team was doing so lousy. We had a great party and the food was superb. Many of the retired members did show up and it was great fun recalling old times. Not once did the fire that I apparently left burning come up in conversation. At about 1:30 a.m. some of the boys started talking about going to a strip club in Revere. This didn't appeal to me. The fire was still on my mind. I felt utterly incompetent, and the beer I had consumed did nothing to make me feel any better.

The following morning I reported for duty and relieved the night chief. They had not left the fire scene until 1:00 a.m. When Eddie, the night chief who had relieved me, said, "We had a very interesting night, Connie!" he did not hear the low moan that came from my mouth. Eddie also told me that the Arson Squad was still at the fire and that they wanted to talk to me. I summoned my courage and asked, "How bad was it Eddie?"

"Hey, Connie, as soon as I got out of the car I could smell the gasoline. The place was really cooking."

Now I was confused. What the hell was going on?

"Connie, you didn't have a re-kindle. The second fire started four doors down from the first fire. Your job was out. But the guy that set the first one was pissed off at you guys so he started another one. This time he used an accelerant."

When we arrived at the fire the Arson Squad was at the scene. They told me that from all appearances the second fire had nothing to do with the first one. It was a family squabble that turned nasty. Money had been loaned and not repaid, and this situations was topped off with a jealousy angle. I was amazed to say the least. The fire had been extinguished, all my doubts were uncalled for. The guy had used gasoline, thus the heavy fire when the first units rolled in. The perpetrator was in custody and had made a full confession. I felt an immense sense of relief.

Mopping up operations were complete and companies were ordered to make up. As we turned onto Cambridge Street, there stood the fish enthusiast. The traffic light was red so we had to stop. He was staring at me in a most peculiar way, as if he were saying with his eyes, "You bastard! You murdered my fish!" Would this damn light ever change! No use. I had to say something. We pulled over to the side and I got out. As I walked toward him his eyes never left me. If looks could kill I was a walking corpse. Explanations were all I could offer. The thought crossed my mind that maybe I should offer to pay for the fish and the cups. When I finished saying what little that could be said, my hand reached out to him. He took it into a firm grip and said, "It's OK. These things happen in life."

That particular fire taught me a lesson: Get all the facts and let the conclusions follow.

A Request

The minute that I picked up the car at Engine 8 I knew there was a problem. The brakes were locking. It was a 1991 Ford Crown Vic wagon. The city had purchased three of them to be used as deputies' cars. Since this type of wagon could also be used to carry equipment, it served very nicely. There was snow on the ground that morning, which made driving the dammed thing even more difficult. As I pulled into headquarters I decided to leave the car on the side ramp and call a mechanic. Just as I was closing the car door, a woman ran towards me yelling. She had a frantic look on her face. Now I could see where she was pointing. The fire was in a seven story brick apartment building. Heavy flame and smoke were showing from the fifth or sixth floors. Using the portable radio I called Fire Alarm. They told me that the box had been received and was being transmitted. The building was only a half a block away on the corner of Broadway and Prescott Street. This area consists of some fairly large apartment buildings and Harvard College buildings, some of which are used as off campus residences.

Leaving the car behind on the ramp, I walked to the fire. Occupants were making a hasty exit out of the front door. The temperature was about fifteen above zero with a light wind blowing. Due to the early hour, many of the occupants were making their way to the street dressed in night clothing. As soon as the radio was clear I advised Fire Alarm of conditions and ordered a working fire. Signal 45 was struck and an additional engine was dispatched to the fire. Now heavy black smoke was pouring from the top floor windows on the Broadway side. I wanted to get a look at the conditions in the rear. When I turned the corner fire was blowing out two windows on the fifth floor. There also was a very heavy smoke condition on the upper floors.

"C Six to Fire Alarm," I called.

"Answering, C Six."

"On the orders of Deputy Chief O'Brien, strike a second alarm. And I want an engine and a truck in Ware Street to the rear of the building."

The division deputy, Kevin Fitzgerald, was soon at the fire and took command of the incident. People were at the windows yelling for help. Ladder 1 was at the front and throwing ground ladders. Engine 1 now advanced a two and a half up the front stairs. This line is very important as the stairs are a main means of egress. Due to the serious threat to life and the extent of the fire, Chief Fitzgerald wasted no time ordering a third alarm. Ladder 3 was ordered to ladder the fourth floor rear window and assist occupants to safety. Engine 2 laid a big line and advanced up the rear stairs. The Rescue Company, following Engine 1's advancing line, made the fifth floor and started a primary search. Later, when more lines were in position, a secondary search would be made. Rescue called command and reported that they were encountering heavy fire conditions on the fifth floor. Additional lines were advanced to back up those already in operation. Ladder 1 and Engine 8 checked for possible fire extension in the walls of the sixth floor and found fire in two rooms. While searching the fifth floor members of the rescue squad found a young child. The engine company with the rescue was advancing a line down the hall and was encountering heavy fire in the ceiling and walls. The smoke was down to the floor and hot. Eddie Friel found the little boy. Speaking through the face piece of his mask he yelled to the other Rescue members that he had found one. Paul Murphy was trying to locate a window that he could take out so some air could get in there. The lieutenant of the engine company out in the hallway was now yelling, "It's getting ready to blow!" A hot air backdraft was about to happen. The fire in the ceiling was darkening down and becoming black and hot. Many times these explosions are hard to predict; when one does occur the results can be devastating.

    The engine men were now backing the line down the hall and yelling "Get out fast!" to the Rescue guys. Eddie held the still form of the little boy to his breast as he and the other members of the Rescue team crawled back down the hall. The engine crew had the line over their heads when it blew. They all felt the rush of superheated air as the explosion occurred. Eddie was on the stairs to the third floor when the blast of flame passed over his head. He used his body to shelter the little form. The other Rescue men were right behind him. The engine guys never left the line. Using a fog pattern, they were able to hug the floor and let the heat and flame pass over their heads. At a time like this, experience pays off in a big way.

    As Eddie exited the front door he was giving mouth to mouth resuscitation to the still form. There were no signs of life. This moment is probably the most difficult in the career of a firefighter. The little boy was about three years old. Eddie passed the boy to Firefighter Edward Morrissey, who contined to give the boy mouth to mouth. As the Rescue truck pulled away they were still desperately trying to save him.

    Third alarm companies advanced additional lines and the fire was controlled and then extinguished. A search was made of the entire structure and no other victims were found. I returned to headquarters and started to catch up on a few phone calls relating to some of my administrative responsibilities. The next call was from Dr. Johnson at the Cambridge Hospital; he wanted to talk to someone about the boy who was DOA from the fire on Prescott Street. The request was relayed by radio to the deputy in charge of the fire. Later that afternoon I was informed of the following scenario: the police had called the hospital and said that the baby's aunt had called and told them that the mother had the AIDS virus. Apparently, the fifth floor was being used as some sort of a day care center. The mother had dropped the little boy off that morning on her way to work.

The problem now was that one of our men had been exposed to infection. The hospital wanted to test a sample of the baby's blood. When the distraught mother arrived at the hospital she was asked by a doctor for permission to conduct the tests. She positively refused. Fire Prevention also made a request, explaining the importance of the test. This was also to no avail.

The little boy was waked in the Cambridgeport section of the city. Arson inspector Paul Sheehan attended the wake in full dress uniform. He knelt down at the closed coffin and said a prayer. The boy's mother was sitting close by watching him. Sitting down beside her he conveyed the sympathy of the department. He then gently went on to explain how every possible thing had been done to save the boy. Her eyes never left his; she was glaring at him. Through eyes swollen with tears she told him in a loud commanding voice, "My sister's a fucken liar. I'll never let them do those blood tests!" Paul sat there in silence. She now went on to explain that her sister was jealous of her and had invented the AIDS story. Paul now took her hand, looked deep into her eyes and said that the two fire-fighters who had given the mouth to mouth was also the fathers of loving families. The firefighters had tried to save the boy and now they needed help.

She put her head down into her handkerchief and cried softly. Both sat in silence for a short while. Without looking at Paul directly she now was nodding her head in approval. Paul had the permission papers with him and she signed. As it turned out the blood that the doctors had taken proved to be negative. The boy was not infected with AIDS. It was never proven that the mother was, in fact, infected. Perhaps it was just another evil thing that one person can do to another in a time of grief. The department never really did find out.

When Firefighters Friel and Morrissey were advised of the test results, they smiled. Eddie Friel shrugged his shoulders and said, "Hey, it's all part of the job." Later we learned that Eddie had never told his wife of his concern, although she did admit that he acted a little strange and for a while their married life changed a bit.

A Noise

There it was again! If only it would stay long enough for me to locate it. Mary first noticed the noise when she was driving home from having her hair done. She said that it was coming from under the dashboard. The only trouble was that it would come and go.

We went to visit friends and on the way it was driving us crazy. During dinner the topic of the noise came up. Barbara, our hostess, said that she would like to hear it. So after the meal out to the car we trooped, and there we were—four grown people, sitting in a car waiting for a noise to start. All is silent, not a sound could be heard. Later in the evening, when it was time to go home, Bill and Barbara were laughing softly as we left the driveway. I am afraid they weren't laughing with us.

We were riding along in silence when suddenly it started again. This time it continued and was still going strong as I pulled into our driveway. "You know," Mary said, "it sounds like a *cricket!*" *Chirp, chirp, chirp.* Yes, it sure did sound like a cricket.

"Gee, Mary, when I was in New York getting Jennifer out of college for the summer break I did leave the windows in the car open at some point."

We looked at the dashboard simultaneously and in one voice said, "We have a visitor under there." Mary gave me that special look and said, "It's going to be cold tonight. His chirp sounds a bit hoarse. The poor thing will be cold and hungry."

All the sympathy she got from me was a curt, "I hope the damned thing freezes solid."

As I unlocked the front door of the house I saw Mary pick some grass and tear it into small pieces. There she was, putting grass on the floor of the car under the dashboard. I just shook my head. The poor little cricket! "Do you want me to leave the car motor running all night?" I called...but I ducked inside the house before she could answer.

The next day I was working. Now I was mad! The cricket had made its last chirp.

It was destined to be a dead cricket! As soon as I could get to it, the problem would be history. There was a can of Raid in the dry room of the station. With my head under the dashboard I emptied the can. It was kind of hard to breathe but I did it. The dammed thing would be dead. I guess the strong smell of the raid made the lieutenant walk into the garage. He said in an inquisitive tone, "Captain, what the hell are you doing?" When I explained the situation he said, "I see, sir," and just walked away...shaking his head. I stepped outside to get some fresh air; the next part of my plan called for sitting in the front seat and listening. This I did. I heard not a sound. I had done it. The cricket had uttered its last chirp.

The ride home after work was uneventful. Not a sound could be heard. I do remember feeling a slight twinge of remorse. What had the little thing done to me? It had a life to lead. They say that they eat other insects. After supper Mary asked me how her little friend was. Not having the courage to tell the truth, I told her that he jumped out when I opened the door at work.

"Well, I hope the poor thing finds its way home," she said.

Then it dawned on me...The corpse of the cricket was not yet found! Mary was now bent down on the floor picking up the grass she picked last night. With my luck, my wife would find the dead cricket and I would be dead next! However, nothing was found. As we drove to the shopping center I had the car radio on nice and low. Maybe on the way home I would stop and buy a bottle of wine. One could never tell.

Chirp, chirp, chirp!

My worst fear was realized. The dammed thing was still alive. Mary said, "Oh it's back! Or perhaps it's another one?" I was saying to myself, Do crickets have nine lives? When I parked the car he was singing his song. Its voice was nice and strong. Mary was out of the car looking for more grass.

The next morning was very cold with a threat of snow. *Chirp, chirp, chirp!* Our friend was back. However, the chirp was very weak. The temperature must be getting to the little bugger, I thought. After dropping Mary off to get her hair done I stopped at Tony's gas station to fill up. Over a cup of coffee I explained my dilemma. He listened patiently as I recounted all that had transpired, then he said, "Connie, let's take a look." We sat in the car and finally he heard it—*chirp* and *chirp*. His hand reached far under the front seat then it emerged with a...smoke detector. He started to laugh, I turned red, and the smoke detector went *chirp*. It was an embarrassing moment. The dammed thing must have fallen under the seat when I moved Jennifer's belongings from her college dorm.

When I told the story to Mary she said, "Oh well, if it had been a cricket we would have let it live."

I said nothing.

A Love Story

The Boston area is blessed with a large Shriners Burn Center. This special hospital is funded by the Masonic Order and dedicated to the treatment of children who have been severely burned. There are cases at the center that would make a grown man cry...maybe because we are firefighters, and children injured by fire are special to us.

For some years the Cambridge Firefighters Relief Association has sponsored a day trip to George's Island in Boston Harbor for some of the young patients at the center. The medical staff at the center has told us that salt air can be beneficial for the kids. Usually between ten and fifteen Cambridge firefighters volunteer for the expedition, and we would take about twenty children. Of course, some patients were so badly injured that they couldn't make the trip, and these kids were treated to a show with clowns, puppets and balloons at the hospital.

For this particular trip we arrived by buses at the Atlantic Avenue boat terminal where the party boat was waiting for us. A few of the children could not walk, and they were gently carried aboard. Then we brought several cases of soda, snack foods and sandwiches on board, and we were ready for the trip across the harbor. The weather was perfect—a nice sunny day with crystal blue skies and little wind.

We had just cast off when one of the four nurses accompanying us informed us that we could have a problem: two of the patients had potential suicidal tendencies. One was a sixteen year old girl who had been burned on the side of her face, arms and shoulders. The other patient was a seventeen year old boy who had burns on both hands. We all agreed that these two would need special watching. Their names were Gail and Marty. We made sure that at least one of us stayed near them at all times—especially if they were near a rail.

The trip down to George's Island was uneventful. We were met by the MDC police who helped us set up and serve lunch. We did have a problem with the yellow jackets that hung around the picnic table. Then I noticed it: Gail and Marty were sitting at the same table, talking. I asked one of the nurses if she thought they were talking about us watching them. She said it wasn't likely. When we had finished eating, the games were started. We had a hoop toss and a few other events for those who could participate. It was a great afternoon and everyone seemed to have a good time...and Gail and Marty were always together.

I have to admit, however, that some moments during the day were difficult for me. I remember two boys, about four years old, victims of an accident involving gasoline in a garage. Both boys were horribly burned over the upper parts of their bodies. They couldn't walk and were in a type of wheel chair. I tried to make them smile, did everything I could, but I guess they did not have too much to smile about.

When the boat arrived to take us back, we loaded up to leave, and Mary and Gail were still arm in arm. The trip back to Boston was a little choppy, but the kids were good and none became ill...although, a couple of the firefighters looked a little green to me. Then it happened. Our love birds were missing.

Harold had been keeping an eye on them but somehow got distracted. No panic—we didn't want to distress the other children. The very first thing I did was walk toward the stern and look into the water. There was no sign of them. Now the panic began to build as I wondered if they'd acted on their suicidal tendencies. Then, very coolly, Harold came up behind me and said, very quietly, "Connie, I found them." Our racing hearts slowed down and we all uttered a silent prayer of thanks. I followed Harold to where Gail and Marty were sitting close together and looking out at the sea. They didn't notice us and were never aware of the concern they had created.

It had been a good day. We received many tired but happy smiles. The last I saw of Gail and Mary, they were boarding the bus for the trip back to the hospital. I don't know what became of them, but I hoped that one afternoon of sunshine was sufficient to kindle a spark of love and hope that would give them peace.

A Tug of War

For many years there have been various charitable causes that the fire service has assisted. One of these is the Muscular Dystrophy Association's drive for funds. Each year the departments throughout the country conduct fundraising efforts such as the "Fill the Boot" campaign. Usually a table is set up outside the fire station and people are encouraged to fill the boot with money. Firefighters have stood in busy traffic intersections and sought contributions from their captured audiences of stopped motorists. One year we decided to do something different. We would have a tug of war between the Boston and Cambridge Fire Departments. Someone came up with the idea of stringing a rope across the Charles River, which narrows to about fifty yards at a point between the Brighton section of Boston and Cambridge. There is a VFW on the Cambridge side and we had permission to use the parking lot for a cookout.

The big day finally arrived. It was a beautiful Saturday in August with clear skies and temperatures hovering in the low eighties. You could not have asked for a better day, and we were confident the event would be well attended. The press and the radio station on the Boston side said that they would be there. All was ready. Local merchants had graciously donated hot dogs and hamburgers. Many of the guys had their families with them. This was to be the event of the season!

The Boston boys had mustered a prize crew. It was common

knowledge that their anchor man weighed in at a commanding two hundred and fifty pounds. It was also said that their average weight was about two ten. There would be about twenty firefighters per team. The committee had decided that it would be better if everyone ate first. I thought this a good idea as, frankly, they outweighed us by half a ton. The Boston department is noted for their fine firehouse cooks.

One of the guys had hooked up a sound system and I was selected to do the "tug by tug" announcing. We had the donation boots set up at the entrance to the parking lot. In order to park you would have to put a little something in the boots for "Jerry's Kids". Various companies and businesses had placed wagers on their hometown team, and all money would be donated to the MDA. Everyone was excited! Across the river and through the trees we could see the red lights of the apparatus that Boston had brought to the festivities. After the contest and our sure victory, we could go over to the other side and take a look at their brand new heavy duty rescue unit.

The rope was stretched and all team members were in place. The first team in the river would be the loser. The Metropolitan District Commission police had stopped all boat traffic on the river while the competition was in progress. The air horns on a piece of apparatus gave the signal to start pulling. Almost immediately the Cambridge team moved back about six feet. The Cambridge crowd cheered. The boys on the line were doing great. Before long we would have all those Boston jakes in the murky river and we would be the winners. From where I was standing I could hear them grunting as the crowd was pulling hard for them. They pulled and pulled. Yes! We were getting the upper hand now. Our team muscle was clearly moving back now...tortured step by tortured step. Wait a moment, something is amiss. What on earth is afoot? Our gallant lads are being pulled *toward* the river. It was like some fantastic, unnatural, strong force was suddenly on Boston's side. Then it happened. I could not believe my eyes. Our brave mass of beef was tumbling into the river. One by one our gallant heroes were taking a dive. One of the judges on our side was observing the Boston team through field glasses. The tugging jakes on the Boston side had tied the rope to the bumper of the new heavy duty rescue. He further observed that the truck was moving ever slowly back as the driver sat nonchalantly looking out the window!

After due protests were filed it was decided the tug of war would be a draw and the real winner would be the Muscular Dystrophy fundraising drive. The Boston boys came back over to our side and we all enjoyed the remainder of a wonderful day as the sun slowly set in the west over the tranquil and peaceful river.

The Worcester Fire

I was at a Christmas party when I heard the news of a major fire burning in Worcester. At first I gave it no attention. The city of Worcester has a high incidence of fire; it is an old city and the members of its fire department get their share of work.

When I left the job in 1993, one of the techno-trinkets I kept was my pager. With it I am able to stay informed about fires in the greater Boston area. My sons, Michael and Neal, both are on the job in Nashua, New Hampshire and I get reports on their action. I also get major news stories breaking anywhere in the country. The pager was now broadcasting that the fire was two alarms. Still of no great concern; a chief officer might sound a second alarm for a number of reasons. He could have the makings of a major fire and want the extra manpower. Sometimes you can run into a real smokey fire that will need frequent relief on the lines.

We had just finished the main course when the pager started to vibrate again. The fire in Worcester was now four alarms—with firefighters missing. This is a notification every man or woman in the profession of firefighting fears. The same feeling of comradeship engulfs you and anyone else who does the same type of work.

The party was proceeding along nicely. A Yankee Swap was in progress. Everyone had brought along a small, inexpensive gift for the exchange. My mind was not on the party. It was with the firefighters in Worcester. When Mary asked me why I was pulling the pager out of my pocket, I told her about the fire in Worcester. A somber look came on her face. She asked if it was serious, and I told her that I had the feeling it was. The first report was two men missing, then later it was confirmed that six were missing. The remainder of the party is lost to my memory; my mind was in Worcester.

The following day the news was full of information about the fire. Six firefighters were, indeed, missing. The fire had been in an abandoned warehouse. When the Worcester companies arrived on the scene, there was a report that people might be inside. Those are the magic words—*human life.* The search for human life always takes precedence over the preservation of any kind of building. This is automatically attempted, even if the search will place firefighters in jeopardy. Whether it is a small volunteer fire department or a big city fire department, the members will make every effort to save lives. This is our sworn duty and this is what we do.

When the report came in that two firefighters were missing, a rescue team of fully qualified firefighters entered the building to search for their brothers. They also became casualties.

People who aren't in the business need to understand that when you are in a building such as this, conditions change quickly. Vision can be excellent one minute, and gone the next. Structural changes can and will occur very rapidly; in many cases without warning. It is very easy to become disoriented. You are working with a limited amount of air. The wrong turn can cost you your life. I have experienced the terrible feeling of panic and was lucky to get out. These six men were true soldiers in smoke who did their duty to the very end and met their fate bravely.

A full investigation is in progress, but what really happened inside that building may never be fully known. However, the purpose and dedication to duty these brave Worcester firefighters possessed is perfectly clear. It has been written that there is no greater gift than the sacrifice of one's life for a friend. All firefighters are the friends of all people. They have demonstrated this love to serve over and over again, and as I write these words—and as you read these words—somewhere a firefighter is answering an alarm to enter into mortal combat with fire. It has been that way since the beginning. As firefighters, we do not look for medals or public praise. We do have the peace within our hearts about the job that we love, and when we close our eyes for the last time, we can whisper that we did our best.

About the Author

Connie O'Brien was a member of the Cambridge Fire Department for over forty years; he joined the department shortly after his discharge from the Navy following World War II and worked his way up through the ranks during the next four decades before retiring as a Deputy Chief in 1993. He and his wife live in Arlington, MA. *Facing the Flames* is his second book.